Cover Art

Les Dentelles de Montmirail are vertical jagged outcroppings of white Jurassic limestone which rise behind the wine village of Gigondas. This geological anomaly is visible for kilometres and is a landmark in the southern Rhône Valley.

The outcroppings are named after the French word for 'lace'. While they look solid, in fact they are so thin that in places holes pierce the limestone so that hikers can look through and into the next valley.

PROVENCE

je t'aime

GORDON BITNEY

Illustrated by Paul Dwillies

GRANVILLE ISLAND PUBLISHING

Library and Archives Canada Cataloguing in Publication
Bitney, Gordon, 1940-
Provence, je t'aime / Gordon Bitney.

ISBN 978-1-894694-65-0
I. Title.
PS8603.I885P76 2007   C813'.6   C2007-906889-8

Illustrator: Paul Dwillies
Editor: Christine Laurin
Proofreader: Neall Calvert
Designer: Rebecca Davies Design

Granville Island Publishing
212–1656 Duranleau
Vancouver BC • Canada • V6H 3S4
www.granvilleislandpublishing.com
604.688.0320

Printed in Canada January 2008

The author may be contacted at
provencejetaime@telus.net

This book is dedicated to
Marie-Hélène

Acknowledgements

This book would never have been written except for the suggestion of Tom Johnston, and then the enthusiastic support of my wife, Marie-Hélène. The first outline of the story was read by Nancy McNeill, who said she wanted to read more. Eileen and Paul Dwillies and Lucie Desrochers made their full share of contributions, and I thank David Freeman for his sense of humour.

Finally, I received endless support and encouragement from the publishing team of Jo Blackmore, Victoria Gibson, Christine Laurin, Neall Calvert, Lauren Ollsin and Rebecca Davies to bring the book together.

Introduction

We visited Provence to see friends who had recently purchased a stone house in a charming village. The trip was meant to be just a vacation. However we enjoyed ourselves so much that we returned the following year, possibly to get it out of our systems. In fact we found the area even more interesting and beautiful than before. By the third visit we were looking at real estate. Our lives had been planned and we could see well into the future as to what we wanted . . . or so we thought. Provence changed that permanently.

We bought a house even though I was still working and couldn't be out of the office for more than three to four weeks at a time. That meant my wife took on the challenging task of managing most of the renovations as well as decorating and furnishing the house. Fortunately she had retired and moreover spoke French fluently.

Marie-Hélène survived it. I took longer and longer vacations and then finally retired as well.

Our lives had been turned upside down, our plans reorganized, and we loved it. We travelled extensively in France and couldn't wait to get into the car to see another village, Roman ruin, aqueduct or vineyard. Italy and Spain were within an easy day's drive, and the TGV could get us to Paris in a morning. The wine cellar grew and our tastes broadened. We made an effort to visit every famous restaurant from Léon de Lyon in Lyon to Pic in Valence. Oddly enough it was the small local restaurants with no Michelin stars that most impressed us. It is worth saying that Provence is still growing on us and in our hearts.

PROVENCE, *JE T'AIME* is a story based on the things we saw and did.

—Gordon Bitney

PROVENCE

je t'aime

Gordon B...

Arrival

Our home in Provence

A BANSHEE-LIKE CRY brought us upright and awake. It was followed by confused hissing and screeching and the sounds of chaotic scrambling at the foot of the bed. Furious scratching of claws across the tiled floor and out the open door onto the balcony had us on our feet to investigate.

"They're at it *again*," said Marie-Hélène.

Dawn had barely arrived, but it provided enough light for us to see Tabitha standing aggressively at the edge of the balcony with her tail thrashing, gazing fiercely down the olive tree at another cat descending rapidly to the ground. The ear-splitting shrieks were being replaced by quiet, deep growling, which suggested the row was at an end.

"Well, at least Myrtille didn't bring in any live mice last night," Marie-Hélène said as we returned from the balcony to the bedroom.

"I thought they might have learned to get along with each other by now."

"I think you're still dreaming. After the fights between those two last summer?" . . .

"I'll make the coffee."

French doors in the kitchen opened onto the balcony, where Tabitha was now sitting with her tail twitching back and forth. I walked out and stood next to her at the railing. In the cool and now calm, if not peaceful, morning air, the pale blue sky was crisscrossed with contrails from jets making early morning flights. The sun broke over the hills to the east, spreading light in the valley. Aside from a cock crowing in the distance there were no sounds—so different from the constant city traffic in Vancouver.

The previous day we had travelled from Vancouver to Lyon, a twelve-hour flight, and then driven for two hours from Lyon to our house in Nyons. We arrived at four in the afternoon, which, with the change in time zones, was then seven in the morning Vancouver time. In effect we had lost a day's sleep. After having stopped to buy groceries en route, then carrying in the luggage, opening the shutters and letting Tabitha out of her travel cage to reacquaint herself with the place, we had had a bite to eat and gone to bed early. The weather was warm and the house needed airing, so the windows and balcony doors were left open during the night.

Marie-Hélène pulled at the fridge door and reached inside to lift out bread, eggs and bacon. This was not going to be a typical French breakfast, but we needed food to help us adjust to the time change and to ease our travel stress. We had learned that not eating properly only made the process more difficult.

The blue sky was glorious compared to the dull grey clouds of Vancouver in April. I walked onto the balcony and looked over the railing to see Myrtille, the neighbour's cat, at the base of the tree looking up. Tabitha emitted another growl.

4

"Myrtille wasted no time finding out that we were here," I said, trying to make conversation out of the situation.

"Since we made this her home two summers ago, she must feel she has property rights ahead of Tabitha."

That was too true. Myrtille had moved herself in, and then won us over with her affectionate ways and loud, demanding cries for food. She was a demonstrative thing. Acting at first like a lost waif, she later wouldn't leave, and brought gifts in the form of mice and birds in the middle of the night. Unfortunately some were still alive, and they would turn up hiding behind furniture over the next few days.

It took nearly two months to establish where Myrtille had come from. A couple came walking by one day pushing a baby carriage and asked if we had seen a cat. After listening to their description of *"une petite siamoise, beaucoup de miaow-miaow,"* we produced Myrtille, who had at that moment been sleeping on our sofa. Apparently she had gone missing just days after their new baby came home from the hospital. Our house was on the hillside and her owners' villa turned out to be just at the foot of the hill.

We would become friends with Yvette and Gilles and have apéritifs at each others' homes from time to time. Gilles made a joke of the situation by saying that Myrtille would spend her *vacances d'été*, or summer vacation, at our place, then return home in the fall when we left for Canada.

The problems started when we arrived with Tabitha the following spring. Territorial warfare began occurring at all hours of the day and night. There were times we felt we were living in Lebanon. Rescuing either one or the other eventually seemed futile so we gave up and left them to sort it out—which didn't happen.

I turned on the gas burner on the stove and began to boil water to make coffee.

"The house looks great," I said, searching for a tablecloth and plates. "Let's eat on the balcony."

"In our *pyjamas*? This isn't the Riviera, where nude bathing is okay. This is Provence, and they are plenty conservative here. All the drivers going by on the road below will stare at the open shutters."

"Live dangerously," I said.

"Thanks, I'll change. They can laugh at you," Marie-Hélène added drily.

I moved the iron patio table and chairs we had stored in the living room over the winter onto the balcony and set the table. A car drove by and I could see the driver looking up at me. Feeling self-conscious, I went inside to unpack a T-shirt and a pair of shorts.

Coming back, I looked over the open kitchen and living space we had created. A dividing wall had been removed between the rooms, so that the sun and fresh air streamed through the two sets of French doors that opened onto the balcony. Eating outdoors is one of the pleasures of living in Provence, and we took full advantage of it. The awning over the balcony was as much for protection from the harsh summer sun as for rainy weather. With it extended, the balcony was like another room, only outdoors.

The house and garden had been a work in progress since we purchased it from an old widower. He had built the house and raised his family here. He stayed a few years after his wife died, but lost interest in the day-to-day upkeep and gardening, so he put it on the market and moved to an apartment in the village.

When we first saw it, the house had been unoccupied for some

time and needed a lot of attention. Marie-Hélène had thrown herself into the job that spring with amazing energy. Wallpaper covered every wall and even some of the ceilings. The bathroom was dark brown. We disliked wallpaper. It all had to be stripped off and the walls washed, sanded and then painted. She did this alone, or at times with the help of visiting friends. I returned to Vancouver to manage my law practice.

In the midst of the work, Marie-Hélène's friend Jane arrived on her vacation. A natural decision maker, she saw the scale of the work ahead and put herself in charge. She started by walking through each room with a paper pad and pen and making long lists of the things that had to be purchased. She looked at the curved mouldings on the ceilings and said that stencilling would act as an attractive transition between the wall and the ceiling. Stencils were added to the lists.

Marie-Hélène had wanted to paint several pieces of old *provençal* furniture. Jane said no. When Marie-Hélène persisted, Jane carried the pieces outside, stripped away the aged varnish and then waxed the wood. Marie-Hélène was first taken aback, then delighted when she saw the inlaid wood details.

Jane had enormous energy and worked tirelessly. Once, after a week of ceaseless work, she saw that Marie-Hélène was exhausted, so she told her to put down whatever she was doing, because they were going out for the rest of the day to relax.

Between the two of them the work had moved along quickly and efficiently. The next summer Marie-Hélène had renovated the kitchen, and this year we had plans for a guest suite on the *rez-de-jardin* or garden level.

"After breakfast I should telephone the Drouins next door. They'll have seen our car by now and know we're home."

"Okay, I'll bring in the rest of the luggage."

Breakfast on the balcony meant looking at the garden, so when we were finished eating we began the process of settling in by pouring more coffee and taking a walk outdoors in the morning sun.

We had dreams for the garden, including setting a stone bench in front of an old stone wall with rich-scented blue lavender planted at each end, and building dry stone walls to improve the paths. Everything required time and money, neither of which we had in great supply.

The long-neglected and overgrown garden had needed weeks of weeding, pruning and replanting when we arrived. We both loved gardening, though, and this one grew on us the more we tended it. We wanted a *provençal* garden that would attract bees and other insects, so we visited a *pépiniere* and bought lavender and valerian. We tore out the meagre and neglected patches of grass on the level areas beside the house and replaced them with several truckloads of crushed gravel, to create two patios. The rest of the property sloped down to the road and had grown wild for some time. The slope gave the house elevation, so that we overlooked the red tile roofs of the village of Nyons and the forested mountains that surround it. These mountains shelter the village from the harsh mistral wind in the Rhône Valley and hold the warmth of the sun in winter, giving Nyons a better climate than the surrounding area and the nickname *Petit Nice*.

We sipped our coffee while inspecting the condition of each tree and plant, first by the house and then down the slope on what remained of the old garden paths. Returning to the house too early meant getting down to the work that needed to be done, so we lingered, sitting on a wall and talking, pulling at a weed or two—having a time-out.

We learned in Provence how to create all sorts of time-outs.

One was with a bottle of *rosé* wine, fresh from the fridge, that would be put on the table at lunch. We rarely drank it in Vancouver. However, it made a perfect fit in the dry climate of Provence. We bought various Tavel *rosés*, and then on long, warm afternoons sat in the garden sipping and offering personal opinions about how they compared. These wines are born of a hot climate and soils of limestone, clay and quartz stones. This permits the winemakers to fashion from a half-dozen varieties of grapes a wine with structure, solidity and density capable of power and mellowness, yet retaining intense floral aromas and touches of fruit. The exceptional freshness and vivacity of a Tavel was a delight on hot summer days.

A screeching sound emanated from near the house. Tabitha must have ventured into the garden and met Myrtille.

"I suppose unpacking is in order," Marie-Hélène said somewhat wistfully, and we walked back indoors.

Tabitha was a veteran traveller who journeyed in her own bag that I placed under my plane seat. She had turned up the first time in our garden in Vancouver as a kitten visiting from the neighbour's yard. Her appearances became more frequent, and one rainy day she arrived at our back door asking in. We fed her and then she settled in to explore the house.

"She doesn't purr," Marie-Hélène observed.

"She may not know how," I offered. "Her owners ignore her."

As the summer passed, the kitten learned how to visit at night. She climbed the trellis giving access to the roof. We were in the habit of leaving the balcony door to the second-floor bedroom open for fresh air. One night we felt the slight thud of a weight landing on our bed, followed by a faint "Che-r-r-up?" Then the kitten walked up to the head of the bed and pawed at the covers. One of us lifted the sheets. She crawled under, then pushed her way to the foot of the bed where she slept for the rest of the night. Marie-Hélène, a born animal lover, was won over.

Tabitha continued her visits over the summer and into the fall, coming and going at her pleasure. Then, late one cold fall night, Marie-Hélène woke up, saying she heard a noise. "I heard thumping sounds on the roof and then a cat crying." We opened the balcony door and the cries grew louder. The balcony and the railing were coated with hoarfrost. In the eavestrough several feet below was Tabitha. She couldn't seem to move, and her cries became desperate when she saw us.

"She's hurt and we can't reach her down there!"

Marie-Hélène looked around and saw an area rug on the floor. She picked it up and draped it over the railing until it reached the cat. Tabitha dug her front claws into the rug and tried to climb it, but without success. We slowly pulled the rug up until I could take hold of her and lift her over the railing.

"She must have slid down the frost on the shingles and landed in the eavestrough."

I carried her into the bedroom and put her down on the floor. Her rear legs collapsed. "Look—she can't *walk*." I exclaimed.

She attempted to stand up, but her hind legs wouldn't support her. I lifted her onto the bed. Marie-Hélène got some cat treats and the kitten avidly ate them and soon began to purr loudly. One leg was scraped almost to the bone. She just lay on the bed, eating and purring.

At the vet's office the next morning we were informed she had a broken hip. The bones were so small surgery was out of the question. The prognosis for recovery was "fifty-fifty."

Tabitha needed a place to rest and recover, so we folded a

blanket on the floor next to our bed and set out bowls of food and water as well as a makeshift litter box. For days she stayed there, moving only when necessary.

Once up and around, Tabitha again spent her time between our house and the neighbours. The hip had healed so well it was difficult to tell she had been injured. Then one day moving vans arrived and the house next door was emptied. She was left behind.

Chapter 2

Connecting with our French tradesmen

SPRING BROUGHT A FRESH QUALITY TO THE AIR and we had arrived in time to enjoy it. The fields were still grey and leafless—green had not yet begun to transform the hillsides—but the buds were swelling and the days growing longer. The cicadas, or *cigales* as they are known in Provence, were months away from their raucous song. When the cats were apart a certain calm took over.

In the house the long campaign to remove wallpaper marched on. The last room on the ground floor would only give up its paper in inch-sized bits after tedious labour.

Within a couple of days we had settled into our routine, and it felt like we had never left. At the end of each day we celebrated our efforts with a glass of wine on the balcony. On particularly still nights we could hear the church bell in the village ringing out. It rang twice, in case someone didn't hear it the first time. The cock down the hill crowed at dawn and whatever other time he felt like doing so.

We had telephoned several tradesmen and sooner or later they would appear to change the rhythm of our peaceful days. The farmers would bring out their equipment and drive up and down the hills preparing the vineyards and orchards for the growing season, and life would return after the winter interlude.

By the third day our jet lag had receded and the trades had begun to turn up at the front door—not always at the agreed-upon time or the right day, but at least we had the pleasure of knowing they were thinking of us.

The road winding past our house provided a means for getting to know the people who lived in the area. A small red Renault swung out of a driveway just up the hill and sped down the road in my direction. Out of normal courtesy I waved. The driver braked to a sudden stop in the middle of the road and jumped out of the car.

"*Bonjour, bonjour! Vous êtes arrivés pour l'été?*"

It was Faustin Buisson, an elderly man who in the past had waved at me but never stopped. So these few words were the first to pass between us. He had a small and wiry build topped with a balding head of sparse grey hair. He grinned broadly, exposing a gold canine in a row of crooked teeth and looked me straight in the eye while shaking my hand.

"*Oui, nous sommes ici pour six mois maintenant,*" I replied.

"*Ça c'est bien,*" he said enthusiastically, and then finished with, "*À bientôt.*"

As quickly as he had arrived, he jumped back in his car and sped away. I had seen Faustin coming and going the previous year. I knew nothing about him and I assumed he lived alone, as his manner was that of a solitary person. There was always a sense of scurrying in his movements. Each morning he drove to the village and then returned a little while later.

One day later that spring I met him at the village square and said hello to him, but he showed little interest. This confused me at first, then I thought that possibly I had received his one welcome for the summer.

In many of the villages in Provence the farmers, butchers, fishmongers, cheese makers and other merchants arrive at dawn to set up stands and sell their products in the weekly outdoor markets. The village squares, streets and narrow lanes turn into crowded shopping areas filled with noise and activity. This is also a social event where neighbours and acquaintances can greet each other and have a word or two.

Thursday is the day for the *marché* in Nyons and, as this was our first Thursday since returning, we started off early to take advantage of the best selection. Even though the village is within walking distance, we drove in order to avoid the uphill walk home carrying our heavy *paniers* stuffed with food.

Parking was difficult at any time, however with the market stalls occupying the square, vehicles were pressed off onto the narrow side streets and along the riverbank. *Paniers* in hand, we strolled into the square. Each week as the season progressed the fresh produce changed. Sometimes the plan for dinner would suddenly be altered as the produce we wanted was no longer in season or something new had arrived.

It was a joy to be back and take in the market for the first time again. The stalls and the people milling about create a kaleidoscope of colour and activity. We divided the morning into shopping together for the core ingredients and then separating to buy other things. Each square and street has its own smells: fresh fish in one aisle with water running constantly from the thawing ice on the fish, roasting chicken on spits in the next aisle. Leather goods, spices and incense all offered their own aromas.

I headed for the stall where a man was making *paella*, a saffron-flavoured dish of Spanish origin containing vegetables, rice, meat and seafood, while the shoppers waited and watched. Marie-Hélène went off to another square where fresh vegetables are sold and her favourite lady frequently has fresh rabbit. The plan was to meet at La Belle Epoque, have an espresso, read the *International Herald Tribune* and then drive home. I walked the stalls, past rows of clothing and sausage merchants. The *boules* courts were busy so I stopped and watched a few throws, listening to the click of one metal ball striking another. I walked to the *tabac presse* for the *Herald Tribune* and then headed for our rendezvous point.

As I walked up, Marie-Hélène was waiting in the shade of a plane tree. She gleefully waved her basket at me and then held it open to show me the contents. "I got everything we wanted. Madame had three *lapin* thighs and she sold me the best one, but the asparagus looked dreadful so I got some green beans instead. I bought a dozen farm eggs. Do you remember those deep yellow yolks we found so delicious? . . . How did you do?"

I rummaged in my own *panier* to show her the hot container of *paella* and two packages of sliced meats. "I got everything, and luckily I ran into our gardener, François, who says he'll be over tomorrow."

The next day François arrived. We heard his truck rumbling up the road and stopping in the driveway at seven in the morning. We leapt out of bed and dressed quickly to save ourselves from looking like lazy Canadians. He was as reliable as clockwork, and when he said that he would be there *chaque vendredi*, it was the case. Work for him started early and continued after a brief lunch until five or six. For some unknown reason François called me by my middle name, James, so for him I was *"Jeem."* . . .

At the end of April we were anxious to start work on our guest suite. The workers had all been contacted in the weeks before we left for France and had promised that they were available to start the moment we arrived. Everything was a go.

However, we hadn't counted on the month of May. In France some months seemed to have more holidays than work days. So May is either the best month or the worst month, depending on whether you are a worker or an owner trying to get some work done. There is Labour Day, Victory Day, Ascension, Pentecost, Whit Monday and more. Sometimes two such events fall on the same day or on a weekend, thereby cheating the workers out of a day off. This hardly presents a problem, for if a holiday happens to fall on a Tuesday or Thursday, many of the workers take the Monday or the Friday off as well. This is known as a *pont*, or bridge. It was very logically pointed out to us that it would be foolish to break up a holiday with one day of work. We began to realize that May could easily be viewed as a month off, interspersed with a few days of work.

Quite apart from the holidays, there was a peculiar loose sense of time for some of the *provençal* tradesmen that we got to know. Was it safe to leave the house in case that day a tradesman happened to show up, even though for the last three days he had failed to do so?

We created strategies to hold onto the workers until a project was completed. The young man who installed the kitchen cabinets was offered an apéritif and dinner so that he would work to finish the job before he got away that evening.

The mason had said that he would arrive at our place at dawn on Monday, hadn't he? So by noon on Wednesday I called his wife and said that probably with my poor grasp of French I hadn't understood him properly, and could she possibly ask him to call to set another day to start the work. We didn't receive a return call, but the next morning the doorbell rang, and with some curiosity about who was there so early in the morning I opened the door to find the mason standing in front of me.

"Bonjour, Albin," I cried with some delight, while a measure of surprise must have shown on my face. The custom in Provence, even if two people pass each other on the street for the third time in a day, is to shake hands. If one person is lax about extending his hand it would likely be taken as almost an insult or that one was angry with the other. Albin's hand had been half-extended while he watched to see what I would do. I reached out and vigorously shook his hand. This ritual demanded looking each other squarely in the eyes at the same time. I could see him visibly relax and then smile.

"Entrez, entrez . . . Marie-Hélène, Albin is here and I've invited him in!"

Down the stairs to the front door she came almost at a run.

"Albin, je suis ravie de vous voir," she enthused.

He obviously missed the irony in the greeting as he glowed with pleasure and stepped inside. I noticed Tabitha slip past our legs and out the door, only to stop when she saw Myrtille sleeping on the flagstones warming in the morning sun. She quickly changed directions and headed off behind the house.

After exchanging all the necessary pleasantries with Albin, we got down to business. There were several hundred floor tiles that had to be returned to the *magasin de bricolage*, the equivalent to a lumber yard in Canada. Albin had delivered a load of tiles last fall that I had later unwrapped to discover they weren't the ones we had ordered. I put on some work gloves and pitched in to help load his truck. Albin stacked them one on top of another onto wood pallets in the middle of his truck bed.

"Albin, ce n'est pas possible. Elles glissent et tombent," I said, making a sliding motion with my hands to indicate the tiles were piled too high and would fall as soon as the truck was set in motion.

"Pas de problème." he responded casually, smiling at me.

I couldn't see why he thought loose stacks of tiles would be safe to move, but reluctantly accepted that he knew what he was doing—after all, this was what he did for a living. We finished loading the truck and hopped into the cab. As we began to pull out of the driveway a loud crashing noise erupted behind us. I looked at Albin, who eased the truck to a stop with his mouth hanging open.

"Merde!"

Turning to look back, I saw the tiles spread across the truck bed. Albin climbed up and began to restack them, the broken ones on the bottom, the whole ones on top, arranging them more evenly and wrapping them loosely with plastic in an attempt to prevent further sliding. We started off again, this time very slowly. Fortunately the *magasin de bricolage* was less than a kilometre away and we arrived without further incident. Albin waved at one of the yardmen to come over with a loader and move the pallets into the storage shed. We walked into the office where he had the salesman credit his account. He had forgotten about the broken tiles.

Albin didn't stay at the house to do any work that day, nor did we see him for another week. After all, this was the month of May.

"You know," I said to Marie-Hélène over lunch on the balcony, "I think I'm beginning to understand why we've had so much trouble with Albin's work," and I related the whole story to her.

We began to realize the drawbacks of owning a house so far away that travelling there was an event in itself. If the job was left with the tradesmen to do in our absence, they inevitably did it as they saw fit, regardless of our instructions.

In our second week the Thursday market was on, so we left the *maçon* and his crew with specific instructions as to where to open a doorway through a stone wall, and then went to the village to shop that morning. When we returned home, they had marked out with chalk a completely different location on the wall and were getting out hammers and drills to start in. After redirecting their efforts back to where I wanted the door, I asked why they had decided to move it. Apparently they had looked at the wall and thought they had a better idea.

As this was not the first time something like this had occurred—spikes were driven into the exterior stucco while we were in Canada—we put a stop to all work unless we were present to keep a close eye on the progress. This was a sensitive matter, for if they felt they were being watched too closely they would think we didn't trust them—which in fact was true. And if we weren't nearby, they reverted to their own decisions despite all instructions to the contrary. I learned to be very precise about what we wanted, both verbally and with gestures, lots of pointing, and even sketches on paper. Then I'd walk away to do some gardening and just happen to be walking by on the way to find a garden tool. I could look in and congratulate them on their work so far. This strategy seemed to be a successful balance of presence yet distance. Often my very passing at a critical moment resulted in their consulting me on the next decision they were about to make. This turned the work into a joint project with us all putting our two cents' worth in and reaching a consensus before proceeding. It certainly prevented returning to find a hole in the wrong place.

The electrician arrived Tuesday and began installing wiring. Then, at the end of the second day, I saw him putting his tools into his case, so with some concern I asked if he would be back the next day. He reassured me that yes, he would be back, *normalement*. For a moment I felt relieved, and then with growing alarm I began to think about what he had actually said. He'd said, "Yes, I will be back the next day—" So far so good. But then he had added *"normalement."* Slowly I realized what this little addition to the sentence really meant. It meant, "Normally I would be back, but . . ." I had come across that word before. As the French are reluctant to say no, instead they say "yes, normally"—which means "no, definitely."

I smiled at the electrician as he lifted his tool case and headed toward the door, knowing that I had lost him for an indefinite length of time. I wanted to say something more, but I bit my tongue instead.

No one came the next day and it was mid-May. "Let's risk it and drive to Avignon on Monday. Probably no one will turn up and we can at least buy the fixtures."

We needed some bathroom fixtures and decided Leroy Merlin in Le Pontet just north of Avignon was the best place to buy them. Really we just wanted a day's outing.

In sunny weather the drive south toward Avignon is a delight. Along the narrow and winding D538 from Nyons to Mirabel-aux-Baronnies, crumbling stone structures dot the orchards that cover the rolling hillsides. Between Mirabel and Vaison-la-Romaine, vineyards become more prevalent and signs appear indicating *dégustation* for anyone who wants to stop. We had stopped and sampled from time to time; however, we felt awkward taking the wives or *vignerons* away from their work to open bottles for us to taste and then not buy their wine. As a result, we already had a sufficient number of 'guilt' wines that wouldn't cellar long. So we brought them out for unannounced guests before the contents turned to vinegar.

The hills become steeper between Vaison and Le Barroux as the D938 winds along a narrow valley. Then it abruptly descends to the broad fertile plain of the Rhône Valley, where the road straightens and the frustrated *provençal* drivers who have been bottled up behind us in the earlier curves pass at dangerous speeds and disappear in the distance.

Carpentras has no exterior ring road, so all drivers going through have to suffer the congested streets. Then, reaching the south edge of the city and the arrow-straight D942 highway, we dashed to Avignon.

We took the exit ramp at Le Pontet, a suburb on the north side of Avignon, and did our shopping. The drive took less than an hour. We had talked very little on the way as we were preoccupied taking in the scenery for the first time this year.

"We should be able to make it into Avignon for lunch. Do you want to try La Cour du Louvre in town or go to Le Bercail across the river?" Marie-Hélène asked.

"Le Bercail. . . . It's sunny and warm, so we can eat on the terrace by the water," I answered.

Le Bercail is known for its stunning location on an island looking across the Rhône River at Avignon. We arrived to see the bright red parasols that shade the diners spread along the riverbank. A canal boat with a husband-and-wife team and a child playing on deck chugged by as we ordered lunch.

"Bon appétit," we said, and touched glasses. Our conversation turned to the fish and ducks swimming in the river just below us.

We gazed across the river toward the towering walls that surround the old city of Avignon. In 1309 Pope Clement V, fearing the violence and chaos in Rome, moved the Papal Curia to Avignon and began construction of the Pope's Palace, which grew to cover an area of over 11,000 square metres and still dominates the skyline. Our view included the Pont d'Avignon, which now extends just halfway across the river, and its small chapel midway on the remaining part of the bridge. The 900-metre stone *pont*, built between 1171 and 1185, was constructed because of the divine inspiration of a shepherd boy. But unstable soil in the river bed led to numerous collapses, and finally the catastrophic flood of 1668 swept away too much of the structure for it to be worthwhile rebuilding. The shepherd was beatified Saint Bénézet for his vision, and the bridge inspired the song known around the world as *"Sur le pont d'Avignon."*

We returned home that afternoon to find a rumpled piece of paper stuck in the door stating that the mason had been there but couldn't get into the house to do any work. The tradesmen just assume there will always be someone there to let them in.

Marie-Hélène said, "Oh well, it was a nice day anyway."

I had a sick feeling that they had left to start a new project somewhere that someone else had been waiting on, and that we wouldn't see them again until that project was finished in a week or a month, or possibly longer.

•　　•　　•

Our projects kept us from pursuing the things that we had come to Provence to do. We had bought bicycles to get out into the countryside, not in a car but in the *plein air,* as the French call it.

Except for a couple of outings when we first got them, they had remained in the garage. We assured ourselves we would have time to put them to use. Today, as a break from our work, and because no trades were there, we decided to do just that.

I got the bicycles out and pumped up the tires. We lacked the smart cycling outfits that we saw on the main roads almost daily, but we had shorts, runners and T-shirts and that would have to do. We also had something few Frenchmen seemed to wear—helmets.

The hill behind our house offered excellent riding. The back roads that ramble through the hills have almost no traffic except for the comings and goings of a few farmers. We planned a ride some fourteen kilometres over the hilltop to Vinsobres, lunch there and a return at our leisure. The first part of the ride was a steep section to the crest of the hill. This was the hardest part and it left us puffing.

"I need to rest," Marie-Hélène said, climbing off her bicycle.

"So do I," I said, gasping.

We sat on the ground next to a vineyard for several minutes while we recovered our breath.

"How do these vines grow here?" Marie-Hélène asked. "There's just rock and no soil."

I looked around to see vines growing out of a surface covered in stones. No soil was visible.

"Well, there is soil underneath. The ploughs just pull the stones to the surface."

The first few leaves of spring had recently appeared on the vines, and small clusters of buds showed where the grape clusters would follow.

We wiped our brows, climbed back on our bicycles and settled down to the easier ride ahead. From here the road followed the contours of the land. We sped down the ravines to cross small bridges and struggled up the other side of each succeeding knoll. The hilltop has largely been turned into vineyards and orchards, with some undeveloped wild forest. We stopped from time to time on the crest of a hill to take in the stunning vistas south toward Mirabel-aux-Baronnies with Mount Ventoux in the distance, and then north into a small, heavily cultivated valley with stone farmhouses dotting the hillside. Animals are a part of life in this corner of the world. Cats, dogs, chickens, rabbits, donkeys and goats were visible in the farmyards.

We timed the ride so that we would arrive for lunch. What we hadn't considered was the weather, which looked sunny when we started off but rapidly began to change to clusters of fast-moving clouds. In the distance we could make out patches of rain. We had pretty well made it to Vinsobres when one of the clouds opened up overhead and soaked us through.

By the time we descended to the village and rode up to the restaurant we had dried a bit in the sun, but the owner took a long look at us standing at the doorway dripping onto his floor.

"Sacrebleu!" he muttered under his breath, and then to us, *"Restez-là, s'il vous plaît."* Off to the kitchen he went, returning with two towels.

We wiped ourselves down as best we could and then he seated us in the warm sun on the patio. We had tried this restaurant on an earlier occasion but found it closed. The couple who operated it had been away on their honeymoon. Today they were both here, she serving the tables, he seating people. However, they took time to talk affectionately to each other, and catch each other's eye as they worked.

"He keeps patting her butt," I said.

"Stop that," Marie-Hélène said in a lowered voice.

"I'm not the one—"

"Gordon!" she glared at me.

"But . . ."

"Butt nothing!"

Our lunch arrived just then. Mine was a delicious chicken thigh with crackling skin, served with a purée of potatoes, and Marie-Hélène had a lettuce-and-sliced-tomato salad with large shavings of parmesan over the top. A small bottle of truffle-infused olive oil came with it. As we were in a well-known wine village, we ordered a demi-carafe of Vinsobre wine.

On the ride back to our house we managed to dodge any showers and enjoyed coasting down the steep hill that had given us so much work at the start.

Chapter 3
Buying French real estate

REAL ESTATE TRANSACTIONS in another country should be considered a matter of "assume nothing and ask questions about everything." Buying our house seemed an easy enough task once we had found the one we wanted. We had spent two weeks in Nyons with a realtor looking through listings and visiting more than a dozen houses.

We became acquainted with stone ruins advertised as *maison à restaurer*, which meant that there was a lot of work to do and a lot of money to be spent. We had been warned about the amount of money involved in restoring an old stone house. "It's cheaper to build a new house than restore a ruin," was the advice. One house was built into a cliff face so that in rainy weather it offered its own running water across the floor. Another was a villa on the knoll of a hill with fabulous views. Then we noticed that all the trees leaned south from the force of the mistral wind. A delightful *mas* in the countryside had no water supply as the well had gone dry. It was understandably vacant.

Finally, on the flight home we decided to make an offer on a house sheltered on a southern hillside on the outskirts of Nyons. Marie-Hélène telephoned the realtor and then e-mails went back and forth without any documents being signed.

"Don't we need to make a formal offer?" I asked the agent.

"No, it's not necessary," she said.

The next e-mail we received said that the vendor would leave the sinks, the toilets and the kitchen cupboards.

"But those things are fixtures and go with the house, don't they?" I asked, astonished.

No, apparently not, at least not in France. We were told that when someone rents an apartment the tenant must install his or her own fixtures. A vacating tenant takes *all* fixtures.

"What about the doors and the light switches?" I wanted to know.

Well, those things do go with the house, but not the light fixtures, I was informed.

After some further negotiations, the price was agreed upon, but there had been no discussion about a deposit.

"We'll get to that," was the response.

Then two days later the tone changed. The e-mail read, "If you are serious about the house please send us a deposit of ten per cent of the price immediately." We were to learn later that a rival offer had come in from another real estate agency. When we sent our money in the form of a bank draft drawn in euros, we knew we had crossed the line and were committed to owning a house in Provence.

Closing the purchase of property in France proved to be another new experience. Arriving at the office of the *notaire* to sign the papers, we met the realtor, Madame Joule, already there, waiting with the vendor. He was a retired civil servant, in fact the former tax collector for the village. We had been told that his career hadn't made him very popular around Nyons. He was seated in the waiting room like an old curmudgeon and rose reluctantly to be introduced.

The *notaire's* secretary appeared and showed us all into an office furnished with a few chairs and an oversized ornate Louis XIV desk. The *notaire* rose from his antique chair in a grand welcoming manner, shaking our hands. Then his secretary carried in a heavy, leather-bound tome, which she set on the desk in front of him already opened to the relevant page.

He put on his glasses and read the entire transaction aloud to us.

Did we have any questions?

I asked if we would receive a deed to the property. Of course not, was his reply. It was, after all, all recorded in the title book he had in front of him.

Was there a plan of the property I could see?

No, there wasn't, the vendor said. It seemed that when the village expropriated a corner of the lot to put the road through no one had bothered to do a new plan. I saw the *notaire* take the cap off his fountain pen and make a notation in the margin of the tome.

At this juncture the vendor was showing signs of considerable agitation. "Why do you need a plan? After all, the property has a wall along one side and the rest is fenced. Isn't that clear enough?"

I acquiesced to this assertion as there was nothing else to be done short of stopping the transaction. "Any other questions,

Monsieur?" the *notaire* asked. We moved along to the signing of the documents.

We were all handed ball-point pens and the secretary moved the documents past us in succession, showing us where to sign. Madame Joule stayed at the side of the vendor and talked quietly to him to see that all went well. Once the papers were signed, the secretary gathered them up and left the room.

I had been expecting to see a statement of adjustments showing the use of the funds we had given to the *notaire*. Nothing had appeared.

"Do you have a statement for the funds?" I finally asked.

"Monsieur, that will be in the report that will be mailed to you in a few months."

We were handed the keys.

The *notaire* stood up, indicating that the transaction was complete. The vendor remained seated and asked when he would receive his money. That would be in a few weeks, he was told. We all shook hands and filed out of the office.

Marie-Hélène and I had the keys and immediate possession of the house. It was now ours. So, giddy with expectation, we drove over, unlocked the front door and walked in. We looked around at the dusty rooms, peered out the dirty window panes and began to realize the amount of work we had ahead of us. The empty rooms echoed as we walked about. The realtor's *'À Vendre'* sign was still nailed to one of the shutters. We found some dust-covered tools the vendor had left behind and pried the sign loose.

That we were starting from scratch hadn't fully occurred to us. We needed everything: beds, chairs, fridge, stove, dishwasher, cutlery and much more. As agreed, the toilets, sinks and the kitchen cabinets were still there. Fortunately, friends had lent us their house to stay in for the time being.

As every room in the house was wallpapered, we decided the bathrooms were the place to start. We bought scrapers and litre-sized spray bottles that we filled with water and used to soak the walls. The glue softened and we began to scrape and peel the paper. However, it only came away in small pieces. This proved intolerably slow considering the amount of wallpaper to be removed. Then I noticed a four-gallon garden sprayer that had been left behind in the garage. I filled it with hot water and sprayed a strip of wallpaper from floor to ceiling. The entire strip peeled away in a single piece. We began to make progress and moved on to other rooms.

Friends came and went, each contributing labour as well as moral support. They had looked at the condition of the house and knew we needed it. Their enthusiasm helped us continue. All the same, we knew that we had gotten ourselves into far more work than we had thought. Without their assistance we could easily have been overwhelmed and dispirited. We dug in and stayed at it.

Looking around the garden that first spring, I stopped to examine a pile of wood that was infested with a colony of large black ants. The house didn't have a fireplace, so the wood had to go. There was too much to burn in the yard and I had no means of hauling it away. Our neighbour, an observant man, I came to learn, leaned over the fence just then and introduced himself as Monsieur Jean Drouin. We chatted amiably for a few minutes and then he asked, "What will you do with that wood?"

"I don't know what to do with it. It's infested with ants."

"Pas de problème," he said. "It's olive wood and burns very well."

I clued in. "Would you like the wood?" I asked.

In less than an hour we had moved it all over the fence and he had carried it to his garage. The wood and the colony of ants were gone and, with another problem solved, I breathed easier.

That spring I had returned to Vancouver and my law practice, leaving Marie-Hélène to finish stripping the wallpaper and painting. She had also been trying to put up curtain rods, in order to hang drapes. The walls were not wood-frame construction, however, but stone and concrete. The electrician had been using an industrial-sized hammer-drill for boring through the walls, which he lent her. The job involved holding a ten-pound drill that was two feet long at the top of a six-foot ladder. The vibration from the drill made a deafening noise and set everything shaking, including the ladder. When she put the drill down for a moment to rest, Marie-Hélène heard someone knocking. Covered in dust, she opened the front door. It was the neighbour's wife, Suzette.

"Marie-Hélène, are you using an electric drill?"

Marie-Hélène nodded, *"Oui."*

Suzette looked absolutely horrified. *"Mais non! C'est un travail pour un homme!* I'll send my husband down immediately to help you. Please wait."

A few minutes later Jean appeared. "Can I help in some way?"

They spent the day drilling holes in the stone walls, screwing curtain rods up and hanging drapes. That day a close friendship was established. Our neighbours had taken it upon themselves to look out for Marie-Hélène, and so they did. They asked her for dinners, took her away from her work for walks, and offered every type of assistance.

•   •   •

That first spring we made shopping trips for furniture and assorted other things to make the house liveable. Once we had the basic necessities like beds and kitchen appliances, we decided to furnish the house as much as possible with genuine *provençal* pieces. Their simple rustic craftsmanship has a relaxed elegance that immediately attracted our attention. We resisted the detailed and fine antiques, opting instead for furniture that could be used for day-to-day living. The wear and patina only added to their charm.

I came across a small oval-shaped keg with a long leather strap to carry it over a worker's shoulder. He would have filled it with wine each morning which he drank over the course of his day working in the vineyard.

For pottery the village of Dieulefit just north of Nyons was the place to go. It had become a centre for potters because of the fine clay deposits nearby. We drove over to visit the pottery studios scattered along the streets. The variety was astonishing and some of the pieces so artistically made we sometimes bought just for the pleasure of owning them.

Some villages had Sunday *marchés* for antiques and a slew of other goods. We carefully searched through the junk spread out on the sidewalks, hoping to turn up a genuine piece that had been painted or damaged but was repairable. We began to understand that a lot of paint remover, steel wool and furniture wax can often bring back the finish of a unique table or chair made from a rare wood. The seller either couldn't be bothered to do the work himself or didn't recognize what he had for sale. Before buying the house, neither of us had ever guessed that treasure-hunting would become one of our most absorbing pastimes.

There are different qualities of used furniture outlets, selling anything from high-grade antiques to worthless junk. The *antiquaires* sell the real thing at prices that assure the buyer the piece is both genuine and valuable. Then there are the *brocantes*, selling a second tier of quality where old and increasingly rare *provençal* furniture is more likely to be found. We bought a chest of drawers with an inlaid wood pattern.

In the summer, villages hold *vide-greniers* where anyone can come and spread out their goods on makeshift benches or on the ground, to sell anything from old shoes to their grandmother's linen and silver. Often our best buys came from these attic sales. I found a set of old *boules* still in their worn leather carrying case. Marie-Hélène picked out a two-seat wicker *chaise*.

We were told that the gypsies on the outskirts of Nyons were good at recaning. Marie-Hélène drove over to their encampment with the *chaise* and returned the next week to pick it up. The man had done an excellent job, but when she handed him a fifty-euro banknote he had to call his son over to give her the correct change. He couldn't add or subtract.

On weekends the village *marchés aux puces* are places to buy smaller things like bric-a-brac. We tried the *trocs* that sell furniture nobody wants, hoping to find some misplaced bargain, but gave up on their inventories of junk after a few visits.

Never knowing from week to week what might turn up, we returned now and then to L'Isle-sur-la-Sorgue. It is by far the best hunting ground for antiques in the area, and is the second-largest market in France. The merchants share large buildings and their pieces arrive and sell daily. To hesitate buying something expecting to return the next week is to miss out. In all likelihood it will already be on its way to New York or San Francisco by air freight, or in a van operated by Hunter's Humpers headed for

England. I couldn't help but think that at the rate these pieces were selling it was highly unlikely Provence would have any *provençal* furniture left in a few years.

It was at L'Isle-sur-la-Sorgue that we found the *bistrot* Chez Nanne, where we lunched during our Sunday quests for antiques. Located at the back of one of the buildings, it is frequented by the *brocanteurs*. The food is simple French *bistrot* fare, but the patio is trellised and covered with vines. On one side, fish and ducks swim by in the canal. The shaded setting with clusters of grapes hanging over the tables offers a delightful escape from the frenetic Sunday market. In all likelihood the person we had been negotiating with an hour earlier would arrive and nod and wish us *bon appétit* before joining friends at a nearby table reserved for them.

We decided we needed French *provençal* chairs for our dining room. We hadn't had much success until we noticed a set of seven in one of the stalls. This was a rare find. The *brocanteur* wasn't there; the fellow at the stall across the aisle said she would return in a few minutes. We waited, but after some time she still hadn't returned so we discussed moving on. He saw that we might do so and came over.

"She won't take less than two hundred and ninety euros for all seven," he said, asserting his expertise.

Marie-Hélène and I glanced at each other. We had been ready to pay more than that. The price marked on the chairs was four hundred and eighty. I looked at the fellow and feigned some concern.

"We could pay two hundred and fifty, but we can't wait any longer. Can you help us?"

"Beh oui. Je pense," he replied.

I paid him while Marie-Hélène brought the car around and

folded the back seats down. Just as we had loaded the last chair in the hatch of the car a woman came by and stopped.

"Those are my chairs!"

"Oh yes," I said. "The fellow in the next stall looked after it for you and we paid him."

She went off to see him, while we closed the hatch door and headed for home.

•   •   •

Our drives took us an hour north on the A7 Autoroute to Valence for shopping in the boutiques, to Barjac situated deep in the Massif Central for a giant outdoor spring antique market, and an hour and a half south-west on the A9 Autoroute to Nîmes to see the Jardin de la Fontaine and the best-preserved Roman amphitheatre in France. Nearby, the massive 275-metre-long Pont du Gard, part of the aqueduct that the Romans built to supply water to Nîmes some two thousand years ago, rises almost 50 metres over the Gard River.

In Nîmes and Arles, *ferias* with bullfights are still held each year, although they are less violent than they once were. The bullfighters are unarmed, and their goal is not to kill the bull but to snatch the ribbons off its horns. On the other hand, the bull is free to do all the damage it can. Angered bulls have been known to pursue their tormentors over the arena barrier and up into the stands amid terrified fleeing spectators.

We were walking past the amphitheatre in Nîmes when I couldn't resist telling Marie-Hélène a story about a man visiting a city in Spain known for its more traditional bullfights.

"He had an introduction from a friend to a very good restaurant in Barcelona. The *maître d'hôtel* welcomed him warmly when he arrived and showed him to an excellent table. The man accepted the suggestion of the waiter for the dinner. When the *maître d'* returned at the end of the meal to ask if he had found the dinner to his satisfaction, the man said it was excellent, but he noticed that someone at the next table had what looked like a very unusual dish."

I glanced at Marie-Hélène to see if she was listening, and then went on.

"'Can you tell me what that dish was?' 'I most certainly can, monsieur; it was bull's testicles.' The man was very interested now, so he asked, 'I would like to return tomorrow evening and try that. Would it be possible?' The *maître d'* said he would do his best. So the man returned the next evening and as promised the dish he requested arrived and the man ate it. Once again, the *maître d'* returned after the meal and asked if he had enjoyed it. 'Yes I did, but I noticed they were much smaller than the ones you served the other gentleman last night.' 'Well, that is true, monsieur. . . . You see, some days the bullfighter wins, and other days he does not.'"

•   •   •

While Marie-Hélène is fluent in French and has a natural grasp of dialects, I had learned the language in university and could read, write and speak reasonably well—or so I thought. I began to realize that I had a very small vocabulary and that my pronunciation was apparently abysmal. I learned this when the gardener turned to Marie-Hélène and asked, "What did he say?" . . . The French language was going to be a challenge for me.

The Parisian French taught in classrooms does not apply in Provence, where the words run together into short sentences that are delivered with a staccato efficiency. Furthermore, I was faced with a dialect and a mixture of old *provençal* words not found in dictionaries. I was forced to resort to more basic communication—that international language of gesticulating combined with exaggerated facial expressions. So body language took over, and before long I found myself interpreting gestures, the roll of the eyes, and where a finger was pointed. When Albin pointed at a tool and said *marteau* a second time, I reached for the hammer. Before too long the words began to fall into place. Dealing with artisans, however, is easier as there is something to point at. Social conversation is different again. I learned to hear the nouns first and to fill in the words in between later.

I learned *'bof'* quickly enough, as it summarized our gardener's rejection of one of my gardening ideas. It often accompanied or was used in place of a dismissive shrug. *'Merde'* was a categorical dismissal mixed with hints of contempt.

With Albin *'oui'* became *voui*, and *'vingt et un'* became *vantay ay eon*.

'Pas d'accord' meant strong disagreement, while *'beh voui'* seemed to indicate agreement or at least the acceptance of a suggestion.

I had a lingering fear of mistaking the meaning of just one word and it leading to mirth, personal embarrassment or some more serious blunder. I learned there can be a subtle difference in the sounds of two words, but a serious difference in meaning. *Baiser* means either to kiss or to make love, *baisser* to lower. *Poisson* is a fish and *poison* is poison. It was wise to stay away from some words.

The garden took up much of my time. One day I was working on one of the last areas that needed weeding. Long before a motorcycle appeared in sight, I could hear the deep thrum of a powerful engine. I looked up from the rosemary shrub I was pruning, my nose filled with its sharp, resinous scent. The machine came into view as it rounded the bend in the road and I recognized the black cycle and the rider in black leathers and helmet. While I couldn't see his face through the tinted visor I detected a nod of his head and I raised my hand in response.

The motorcyclist continued on by, and then a hundred metres up the road he slowed, moved to the edge of the road and then swung across to make the sharp turn up the driveway to Faustin Buisson's house. Last year I had become familiar with the thrum of this engine and the cautious approach the rider made on the road. I assumed that he must be Faustin's son. In time I learned that he had moved to Aix-en-Provence to find employment. The family farm was far too small to support him and he probably wanted to get away and explore new opportunities not available in Nyons, as so many other youths had done. Like his father, he arrived alone and left alone. However, that was soon to change, and we were to see more of him that summer.

Chapter 4
Hunting for truffles, and my dry-stone folly begins

PIERRE LUC PAYSAN WAS TELLING ME, "I have sold the farm next month." He lived just up the hill from our house. One neighbour called him a *bricoleur* or handyman. *"Il n'est pas un homme sérieux."* In France to be referred to that way was damning. It meant he was a lazy person, someone not to be relied upon. Marie-Hélène described Pierre Luc as drop-dead handsome with a full head of black hair, and his wife as a blonde, blue-eyed stunner from Rochebrune.

A number of non-resident property owners had tried employing him, possibly mistaking his broad good looks for common sense and reliability. But each in turn gave up and moved on to use other workers.

"You have sold your farm?" I asked with considerable surprise, trying to clarify his mixed tenses.

"Non. I have agreed on the price and Madame Joule with the *agence* has a deposit of 60,000 euros from *les Belges.* I sign next month."

Last fall Pierre Luc and his family looked settled on their farm. He had lived there all his life, and had inherited it when his parents died. Now he looked dispirited and unfocused.

"What does Fanny say about this?" I wondered out loud.

"She is the one who wants to sell," he said rather flatly. "There's no money here. She doesn't like my farm or the village life and moved to Paris three months ago and she took our daughter, Violette, with her. So I have to sell and then go too. Maybe I can get a better price. We will see," he said and shrugged.

Pierre Luc shifted on his feet, then nodded his head at me while tipping the ash off his cigarette with one hand and making a waving gesture with the other.

"*À bientôt,*" he said abruptly, and ambled off toward the village with his dog at his side.

I told Marie-Hélène about the news over lunch.

"It's no darn wonder," she responded, shaking her head. "He's a total layabout. He doesn't maintain his vineyard or the orchard, and he never finishes the odd jobs he's hired to do. He's got a wonderful farm and no debt, probably because no one will lend him money. If it weren't for his good looks he would never have attracted his wife."

Dropping her napkin on the table, she went on.

"Even his dog, Fidel, needs attention. Did you notice the dirty fur and constant scratching for fleas? All his effort goes into his clothes so he looks good at the bar with his drinking buddies. He's prepared to squander away a good life and now seems about to lose his wife."

"What do they live on?" I asked.

"Suzette says the government—he gets a subsidy for having a vineyard, and his wife used to make those little *provençal santon* dolls of traditional figures. The sale of santons brought in good money until the tax authorities came around asking questions. She had to either stop making them or declare what they were doing."

Marie-Hélène took a sip of wine to cool off.

"Now, maybe his wife has a job in Paris. . . . Suzette doesn't know."

"He looked pretty dejected," I said, and we dropped the subject.

Over the course of the summer we would see Pierre Luc walk by, always with his scruffy dog, or see him on the terrace of a bar with his usual *amis*.

• • •

The village of Richerenches is situated twenty kilometres west of Nyons, well out on the plain of the Rhône Valley. It is a medieval village, with stone walls built by the Knights Templar in the twelfth century to keep out marauding bands of robbers, and just possibly to ward off the mistral wind that sweeps down from the north each winter. Parts of the medieval wall have been removed to open the old village on four sides. Inside the walls there remain unrestored ruins suffering from decades or more of neglect. The church has a crack running down the centre of the façade caused by the foundation settling in different directions, and long iron rods can be seen pinning the structure together.

The fame of Richerenches extends far beyond its walls, for it is the epicentre of the truffle trade in the Tricastan region, where the truffle unquestionably reigns supreme. A truffle is an underground fungus like a mushroom. It matures in late fall, but unlike a mushroom, which raises a cap above the ground to disperse its spores, a truffle remains underground and is therefore harder to locate and harvest. Often referred to as the *'diamant noir'* for its outrageous price, it commands a huge market of cash-and-carry transactions. These generally take place between trusted individuals. Buyers can also ask someone standing casually in the street on market day during the truffling season.

In March a year earlier, Marie-Hélène and Barb, a friend from Vancouver, had driven to Richerenches to buy a few truffles. They arrived with cash, some knowledge of the different varieties of truffles and a sense of the price that spring. Suzette Drouin, our neighbour, had offered advice, warning what to expect. Marie-Hélène was anticipating a deal with some man loitering in the street with a small sack concealed under his coat. As it turned out, the trade was very active that day and she was not the only buyer there. Possibly the truffle season was drawing to a close for the year and people were buying up the last of the season's produce.

Rather than dealing with one of the men, Marie-Hélène chose a woman who opened her car trunk to reveal a small basket containing *les truffes*. Could she tell if the truffles had metal stuck inside to increase the weight, or if they were an Italian import rather than Provence truffles? Not likely, but the powerful, earthy aroma was very distinct and convincing. She bought three nearly the size of chicken eggs and paid the lady sixty euros per truffle.

A week later Marie-Hélène read a local newspaper report about a truffle vendor in Richerenches who at the end of his day of sales was robbed of a considerable sum of money. He had a dilemma—call the *gendarmerie* and face having to declare his income to the tax authorities, or remain silent. He decided the loss was too much and called the *gendarmerie*.

Because so much money was at stake, truffle hunting had become a very secretive business. Areas of private forests were marked with signs indicating that hunting was *interdit*. That meant no hunting for truffles as much as for wildlife. One extremely official-looking sign barring entry read:

TRUFFIÈRE
PROTÉGÉE PAR LA LOI
ACCÈS INTERDIT
Art. 379 et 381 du Code Pénal
GROUPEMENT NATIONAL
DES PRODUCTEURS DE TRUFFES

Truffles live in a symbiotic relationship with the roots of oak and hazelnut trees. The biggest problem is ferreting out something that grows randomly and remains hidden underground. Both inventive and covert measures are needed. Experienced trufflers know the land so well they have secret truffling areas to return to each winter. However, truffles are fickle and cannot be relied on to be in the same place the next year. Good trufflers learn to look for a barren patch around the base of the trees where nothing grows. The next clue might be a cracking in the dry surface of the soil in the fall, indicating something is growing beneath. The truffler might mark the spot by dropping a grain of wheat in the crack and return in December when the truffles have matured to look for a blade of wheat with hopefully a truffle beneath it.

As a truffle ripens, it gives off a redolent, earthy aroma that attracts flies. Some hunters wait for the days when the air is still and watch where the flies gather. Pigs are drawn to the strong scent, but they like the taste of truffles too much and are hard to control once a truffle is located. Today, dogs are trained to do the same work with a lot less hassle. Furthermore, it looks less obvious to be walking a dog than a pig. However, training a dog, which is not naturally drawn to the scent like a pig, requires special tricks. Some add a trace of truffle to the dog's food. One family we met found a better solution. They train a pup from birth by rubbing truffle butter on the teats of the nursing bitch.

We've had truffles in omelets and in terrine, and had an entire dinner devoted to truffles as the basic ingredient at Guy Jullien's restaurant, La Beaugravière, in Mondragon. But by far the best was simply thinly shaved truffles on toast topped with a drizzle of the marvelous *tanche* variety of olive oil from Nyons and served as a canapé at the home of our realtor.

In fact, varieties of truffle grow all over the world, but the French lay claim to recognizing this remarkable tuber for its culinary worth. They have honoured it in the usual French manner by forming a fraternal society: the Confrérie du Diamant Noir et de la Gastronomie in Perigord. Other Frenchmen, not to be outdone, shortly thereafter formed the Confrérie de la Truffe de Bourgogne in Burgundy and the Confrérie de la Rabasse Provençale in Provence.

As the annual truffle harvest only lasts from December to March, the villagers of Richerenches sought a springtime activity to attract visitors. Now on the last Sunday in May, every *pépiniériste* within 100 kilometres descends on the village to sell his plants. This may be the most extravagant plant sale in the south of France, bringing gardeners in search of the perfect flowers, shrubs and trees needed for their gardens. For one day each year, the ancient stone village transforms into a flower festival.

We arrived early, hoping to avoid the crowds, only to find the roads leading into the village already plugged by parked vehicles. We joined the throng and walked the rest of the way. We were looking for rose bushes.

Hundreds of *vendeurs* with stalls filled with greenery and bright colourful blossoms lined the streets and squares. Even some book merchants had set up tables to sell biographies of famous French writers and books of picturesque *villages perchés*. Every street was crammed with people and all vehicles barred entry. Down the middle, thousands of buyers jostled their way along.

We selected two superb rose bushes over two metres tall, with deep green foliage and already covered in plump red buds just beginning to open. Several varieties of thyme and sage caught our attention, as did seed packets of valerian, since we wanted a garden with the scents of the countryside.

The rose bushes were far too large for the inside of the car, so the drive home was accomplished with the hatch open and the foliage waving in the wind behind us.

•   •   •

By the end of May the spring sun had grown warmer, drawing us to more outdoor activities. I found myself standing and staring at the unfinished patio of the south side of the villa, trying to decide what to do. The villa had been built on a hillside and the area around it had been levelled. Unfortunately one patio was quite narrow before the land dropped away. This made it too small for practical use and too exposed to the eyes of passersby on the road below. The previous owner had begun building a cemented stone wall to stabilize the slope, but it didn't rise to the level of the patio and in the middle a long unfinished gap remained. It had to be raised to the height of the patio and the centre completed to allow us to expand the level area. However, this entailed building a wall over twelve metres long and two metres high.

The quotation I received from a mason to construct a concrete-reinforced wall was so breathtakingly high that the idea had to be abandoned. But it nagged at me every time we tried to use the patio. I kept looking at the area in the hope of finding a solution. Finally I went on drives on the back roads and scavenged stones from the nearby hillsides, loading the trunk of the car and then hauling them one by one around the villa to the patio. I began by setting a line of stones on the ground where the wall should be. It was a ragged-looking string like a row of broken teeth when François arrived to do his usual Friday gardening. He looked at my efforts.

"Non, non. Ce n'est pas correct, Jeem," he muttered, shaking his head with his forefinger next to his chin. *"Pas propre,"* he continued. "It's necessary to place the largest stones horizontally on the bottom. Stones set on end look unstable and are harder to stack. The first course of stones should be dug half into the ground to create a stable base. After that, place the larger stones first and then use the smaller ones to fill in the gaps. The flat ones should be set aside for the top course, so that it will be level."

Then, leaning forward, he moved his hand from the stones on the ground upward and back toward the slope. "A dry stone wall must be built with a seven-per-cent slope into the hillside so that it doesn't topple over. It leans just slightly back to the slope, but not too much. Then it will stay put."

He smiled while he explained this to me, and then asked, "Where will you find all the stones for such a big wall?"

I had no answer, as it had already taken me days to find and move the dozen or so stones he could see. When I looked at my little row, the time and effort required seemed harder than ever to estimate. All the same, I didn't see any other approach.

The cost to buy stones, let alone delivery by truck, was beyond what I was prepared to pay. This project was beginning to seem like it would take years of scavenging.

"Je les cherche partout," was all I was able to say. He smiled at me again, and we moved on to discuss the watering system. I felt deflated by his realistic assessment of my project.

•   •   •

We needed relief from our work and cooking every day, so by June we began to lunch out more often. La Belle Epoque, on the main square in Nyons with its colourful awning inviting people in, is the village's most popular *bistrot*. We tried it and then returned regularly. A *bistrot* is sort of the upscale equivalent of a North-American café or diner. It is common knowledge that La Belle Epoque is the best in the village, and on any day of the week we would find our trades there as well as the mayor. It is always busy with the hum of conversation, dishes and cutlery clattering, and the odd dog under a table growling or barking at another dog close by.

The owner would tell us which table to sit at, and the *menu du jour* was always posted on the chalkboard mounted on the post in the middle of the room. It was invariably the best choice of the day. We got to know the owner and his wife and were treated as regulars. There was only one problem. The portions were far too large. An omelet overflowed the plate, a salad was made for a labourer who had only had a croissant and coffee at five that morning, and the *menu du jour* was hearty and included dessert. We finally gave up and learned to order one dish for the two of us. Undoubtedly the owner looked on us as "the underfed Canadians." All the same, the food was excellent as well as a bargain, and everyone knew it. The owner's wife stationed herself at the cash register and from there surveyed the room and gave orders to the staff. She handled all the bills and received the money when the patrons rose to leave.

We arrived late for lunch one day after bicycling the back roads to find the *bistrot* full. The owner had just turned away two tourists. He recognized us, lifted his eyebrows and then raised his hands palms up in a gesture of helplessness. It looked like it was no use. Then he seemed to hesitate.

"Une petite table?"

He gestured for us to follow him into the courtyard area. There, squeezed between two potted plants, was a small table with only one chair. He looked around for another, saw one on the other side of the courtyard, and carried it to the table held high over his head and the heads of the other patrons. Then he called a server over to set the table and bring menus.

We smiled and thanked him. He replied, *"De rien pour vous."*

It was no wonder we returned again and again.

As we had arrived late, partway through our lunch the *bistrot* was starting to empty. The owner now had more time to look around to see how the tables were doing. Then I noticed a small boy at a table across from us act startled and look around, wiping the back of his neck. A few moments later another child acted the same way. Curious, I watched the owner hide something behind his leg and casually walk away. It was a water pistol. The parents watched as well, enjoying the game but giving nothing away to the children.

•　　•　　•

We had seen a few unfamiliar cats occasionally strolling through our garden, but none had ever come near us. They left as soon as we showed them the least attention. Then one morning during our second summer in Provence, Marie-Hélène had risen before dawn and was curled up on the living-room sofa reading an Inspector Maigret mystery by Georges Simenon. The kettle on the stove had begun to sing, so she lowered the book and looked out the French doors to the balcony. The sun was just beginning to rise.

"Gordon, there's a face in the window looking at me! The mouth is opening and closing, but there's no sound!"

I walked into the room to see a cat staring at Marie-Hélène through the glass door. In fact, they were staring at each other.

"It's just a cat," I responded. "It must have climbed the olive tree next to the balcony."

I walked over and looked at it, expecting it to run off. Instead, I could hear faint meowing. As I opened the door, the cat backed away. Then it walked straight into the room and let out a loud Siamese meow. It was small, with a lithe, beige-flecked body and black ears and tail.

"M-e-o-w," it emitted again, this time in an even more demanding manner.

"She's hungry," Marie-Hélène said.

I reached for a tin in the cupboard, opened it and put half the contents on a plate. The cat followed everything I did, circling my feet, talking. I put the plate on the floor and in quick gulps she ate all the food. I put down more and she promptly ate that as well.

She stayed. She was, we were to learn, "Myrtille."

Areas of her fur were missing and the rest matted. She was very thin so we suspected she had worms. Marie-Hélène insisted we take the motley little thing to the village veterinarian. After a struggle, we managed to get her into a cardboard box and closed the lid. She cried and scratched all the way to the vet's and then once there fell silent and docile. He looked her over and said the fur would grow back, and he gave us some pills for the worms. We asked how much we owed him. He replied that there was no charge for a stray.

Living with Myrtille, who now seemed to have adopted us, required some adjustments. She was a character who loved to dominate any space she was in with her presence. If I sat down she wanted on my lap, where she promptly went to sleep. If one of us was in the kitchen she would wind herself between our legs and talk incessantly. Her being somewhat nocturnal, we would come indoors during the day to find her napping against the pillows on our bed. When Marie-Hélène was gardening under an olive or an oak tree, Myrtille would run up the tree and bat at her moving hat, then run down and roll around on the dry dusty earth. She seemed to revel in our presence and always wanted to be a part of our activities. If another cat entered the yard there was immediate noisy discord.

Myrtille brought us 'gifts' from time to time. These we could have done without, as they were inevitably her catch of the moment from the garden. These were often left half-consumed on the carpet, as I unfortunately found out one night while walking to the bathroom in the dark. The live gifts would turn up in other ways. One day she arrived with an unnatural grin on her face; looking closer, I could see that she had something in her mouth. She walked over to me, opened her mouth and deposited a very small egg at my feet. We were both dismayed and charmed by her antics, and wondered where she had come from. We asked the immediate neighbours, but no one had seen her before.

Chapter 5

Exploring Aix-en-Provence, and dining on bouillabaisse

WE HAD RENTED OUT OUR HOUSE for eight days at the beginning of June and now had to find somewhere else to stay. Aix-en-Provence, situated two hours south of Nyons by the A7 Autoroute, was too far away for day excursions so we rarely visited. We saw this as our chance to do so and rented an apartment in the heart of the old section. Some 130,000 people live in Aix. They enjoy a climate that has an average temperature of 17 °C (63 °F) and a staggering 274 sunny days each year.

Most cities have one market each week, but Aix has large markets on Tuesdays, Thursdays and Saturdays. Everything imaginable is offered for sale, from fruit and vegetables to African knick-knacks and obscure academic books that should be sold by the pound for the paper. There are stalls devoted to antique linens and to undergarments for women of staggering proportions.

The first morning at eight o'clock I walked one block to Place des Prêcheurs to buy fresh croissants. Entering the bakery, I saw the baker sliding a palette of *fougasse* loafs out of the oven. The smell of the fresh-baked bread sent a pang of hunger through my stomach. I stopped next at a *tabac presse* to buy the *Herald Tribune*, and returned to the aroma of Marie-Hélène's freshly made espresso as I opened the door. The eight-foot-tall shutters were ajar and the morning sun streamed in. We sat in the sun at the breakfast table, set with small cups of espresso, jars of jellies, plates of croissants, and read the paper.

After showering in a stall half the size of a telephone booth, we decided to explore Aix. Cours Mirabeau is a broad boulevard lined with plane trees providing shade from the summer sun. At one end of the boulevard is the massive Fontaine de la Rotonde with its stone lions, and, scattered along the length of the street, more fountains bubble with water.

In the south of France, where water is a scarce and therefore precious resource, Aix-en-Provence is famous for its fountains. Paul Cézanne's father created a large reservoir on the slopes of Mont Sainte-Victoire that assured an abundant supply of water to meet the day-to-day needs of the city. Fountains are everywhere and enliven the squares that appeared as we strolled the meandering streets.

Bistrots spread out onto the broad sidewalks. On the weekends there is often entertainment or an event underway. That Sunday, people paraded the length of Cours Mirabeau to the Fontaine de la Rotonde and back again wearing costumes from a multitude of eras. We recognized Louis XIV, a few blonde Brigitte Bardots and an assortment of Darth Vaders. Many historical periods were represented, and each was accompanied by its own musical troupe or a boom-box playing appropriate melodies.

There was a lot to see, so on Monday we continued to just

stroll about Aix, window-shopping at the hundreds of small boutiques, stopping in one of the squares for refreshments, and finding a bistrot under the plane trees for lunch. The constant street activity is contagious. Within the first few days we discovered Les Deux Garçons restaurant on Cours Mirabeau and Café Verdun on Place de Verdun. University students—sitting in bistrots having apéritifs, talking in the streets or hurrying to meet someone—were everywhere.

Paul Cézanne and Emile Zola grew up in Aix and then moved to Paris as friends to pursue their careers. Zola remained in Paris to write. Cézanne returned to build a studio and paint his most important canvases here. On Tuesday we drove to *Atelier Cézanne*, which somehow remains today. It contains all the easels, paint tubes and brushes, furniture and some of the objects that appear in his paintings. Even the paint-encrusted clothes he wore still hang on hooks on the wall. After he died the studio was kept intact by his son and then it was eventually transferred to the University of Aix – Marseilles, which maintains it as an historical site. If he were to walk back into the studio today he could pick up where he left off. Unfortunately, the art establishment of Aix failed to see merit in his work and turned it away. As a result, while Aix is the home of Cézanne, none of his paintings remain here.

We decided on dinner at Les Deux Garçons.

"I'd like to walk over after dark and enjoy the evening," Marie-Hélène said.

"I'll call ahead for a reservation."

Our apartment was on the north side of old Aix, whereas the restaurant was on the south side, but not a long walk away. We thought we knew the route well and set off by the light of the streetlamps, stopping to window-shop and take in the mood of the evening. Within a few turns in the labyrinth of dark streets we lost sight of the buildings we were familiar with, but remained confident we were heading in the right direction. After some minutes, too many for what the walk ought to have taken, we emerged on the ring road. Nothing looked familiar.

Marie-Hélène stopped at a magazine stand and asked where we were.

"Madame, you are on the north side of Aix." We had walked in a circle and were within two blocks of our apartment. We set off again, and to our good luck our table was still there when we arrived at the restaurant.

•   •   •

I wanted to see the deep rocky inlets, or *calanques*, between Marseilles and Cassis. The drive on the autoroute from Aix on Wednesday was very fast and we exited onto a narrow road winding down to the Mediterranean and Cassis, a village without parking, we began to think. When we arrived, drivers were already circling and waiting for someone to leave. We joined the procession and in a surprisingly short time found a stall. It was still spring and the heavy tourist traffic of summer hadn't arrived yet.

Cassis, once a small fishing village, has been 'discovered' and is now a tourist destination. Tourism is clearly the more lucrative business; the boats lined up along the quay are for *calanques* excursions. The bay of Cassis is a bowl with restaurants forming a line of colourful awnings facing the sea and the quay.

"In midsummer the *calanques* are filled with pleasure boats. It gets mad here," the guide informed us. "It is much better to come now when it's still off-season."

Back at the quay just after noon, we looked for a restaurant for lunch. This area is famous for bouillabaisse and we wanted to try it. After looking at the various restaurants along the harbour, all that we could find was fish stew at a place with a red awning and tables all impeccably set with white tablecloths, napkins, cutlery and stemware. The waiter, in black slacks and a white shirt with sleeves rolled up to his elbows to show he was ready for work, greeted us and took our order. When he returned with two glasses of wine he was chatty, so Marie-Hélène said we had come all the way from Canada to try their bouillabaisse. He straightened his back with a look of surprise, "You ordered fish stew!"

"Yes," Marie-Hélène said, "bouillabaisse."

"That's not bouillabaisse. Just a moment." He dashed off and came back a few minutes later. "I had to cancel the stew and change the order. You're in luck, for the catch today had the right fish. Bouillabaisse is a dish for two and will take some time to prepare. We are members of La Charte de la Bouillabaisse," he emphasized. "Let me bring you some more wine and I'll bring the charter as well."

He returned with a bottle of Cassis white wine and a brochure in both French and English. He explained, "This is a charter signed by a group of restaurants to hold bouillabaisse to its true standards. A bouillabaisse must contain certain fish, although there is room for each restaurateur to create his own style once he has fulfilled the basic requirements."

I had read somewhere that serving bouillabaisse is a ritual. The order is placed and the diners know that they will be waiting awhile. This is an event, not a fast lunch. Apéritifs are ordered and consumed. Conversation flows in the summer sun. Then finally, a large tray of cooked fish appears. The waiter proudly points out all the fish by name, thereby making it clear that the right ingredients are there and the diners have not been cheated.

He will then offer to cut up the fish at the table and add the tasty morsels one by one to the broth. Or he will offer to have the chef prepare it in the kitchen and return shortly with the tureen overflowing with broth and fish all infused together.

We read the Charter and sipped our wine. There is a longer history to bouillabaisse than we realized. Basically it is fish stew made from the catch of the day or whatever the fishermen didn't manage to sell. Like so many great French dishes, it started as peasant food and became a gourmet dish. Obviously the ingredients are variable, but the fish are always fresh. One French epicure referred to it as *'la soupe d'or'* for the golden colour of the broth. And so the legend of bouillabaisse was born. But who could say what the correct ingredients are, or which fishing village knows them? It seems that every village and city claims that theirs is the only authentic version and all others are poor imitations. So in typical French fashion, restaurants in villages group together under their Charter to state what are the essential ingredients for bouillabaisse. Obviously, any restaurant that doesn't adhere to these standards does not make the true thing.

Oddly, the name *'bouillabaisse'* derives not from a word for fish but from *'bouillir'* (to boil) and *'abaisser'* (to reduce)—so essentially it is a cauldron of fish boiled down and flavoured until it becomes what has been described as "a magical synthesis." What distinguishes bouillabaisse is not the fish, which is common to any fish stew or soup. It is the unique flavours derived from leeks, saffron, which also gives it its colour, and fennel seeds lending their pungent taste and aroma.

The fish, of course, come from the Mediterranean. There are two types: dry rockfish and oily fish, like eels. Some restaurants add crustaceans like langouste, but molluscs or mussels are not used.

We looked out at the boats in the harbour and sipped our wine, talking idly. The sun was warm, giving the day a pleasant languor. The wait turned into forty minutes and then an hour. We had long since finished our wine when the waiter walked over to the table carrying a very large tray covered in various cooked whole fish. He named each fish on the plate as he pointed it out.

"*Rascasse, Saint-Pierre, Galinette, Baudroie, Fielas, Cigale de Mer and Langouste.*"

I began to lose track of all the names.

"Now, having shown you that all the right ingredients have been used, the chef will prepare the fish and I will be back shortly."

Marie-Hélène looked up from the English version of the brochure.

"So the fish are Scorpion fish, John Dory, Red Mullet, Munkfish, and Conger Eel. The shellfish are types of Mediterranean lobster and crayfish."

Another twenty minutes passed and we had started into a fresh bottle of Cassis wine when the waiter returned with a huge tureen, bowls and a *rouille* sauce. I could see pieces of fish and crustacean floating in the tureen. He ladled large helpings into our bowls. We put dollops of *rouille* on slices of crusty baguette and added them to the broth.

The waiter pointed to the dish of *rouille* and said solemnly, "A *rouille* is basically mayonnaise flavoured with pimento. We make our own using olive oil, garlic, egg yolks, pungent pimento, saffron, salt and pepper. Of course the baguette is crisp, to sop up the broth. And by the way, we add powdered lobster shell to the broth. It is more delicious that way."

He then left us to enjoy ourselves. We looked at each other

and then at the overflowing bowls in front of us. The tureen still looked full. We marvelled at the diversity of its contents, wondering about each delicious morsel. The overwhelmingly inviting aroma rising up from our bowls captured our attention. Every morsel of fish was different from the next. The broth blended the flavours into what one food writer has called "a symphony of tastes."

Sometime between three-thirty and four o'clock we paid the bill and rose from the table. The tureen was not empty, but we couldn't have eaten more even if we had stayed the rest of the afternoon. I had a brochure in my pocket describing what it took to become a signature restaurant in *La Charte de la Bouillabaisse*. On reaching Aix we took a very long walk, exploring more streets, and turned in early. Dining that evening was not even considered.

On Thursday our walk took us past the famous and infamous buildings of Aix. Place d'Albertas in the heart of Aix has significant historical importance. The place is paved in small, round, uneven stones and has its own fountain. The *marquis d'Albertas* built one of the most beautiful gardens in the countryside nearby. It is open to the public and rivals the garden in Nîmes built centuries earlier.

Louis Mercoeur, *duc de Vendôme,* the governor of Provence and a cardinal of the Church, fell in love with a woman and built a folly where they could meet without attracting unwanted attention. The *pavillon de Vendôme* was designed with a portico that carriages could roll under to disgorge the passengers unobserved at the base of a stairway leading to the upper floor, which consisted solely of a bedroom, a water closet and a salon. Walls and gates closed off the garden from outside view.

Pablo Picasso had been living in Perpignan when he learned of a château near Aix that was for sale. It was the château at Vauvenargues under the north flank of Mont Sainte-Victoire. The marquis needed money. Picasso drove over, and when he looked down from the village at the beautiful building and into the courtyard surrounded by pine trees he decided to buy it. However, the very vantage-point over the château that sold him on it would in time bring him to hate the place, for the tourists could stand there with binoculars and cameras waiting for him to step out-of-doors. Even though he pursued his fame as an artist with passionate intensity, he remained a private man living almost entirely within a close circle of friends.

The next day we took the D10 east from Aix along the north side of Mont Sainte-Victoire to see the château from the same spot Picasso first saw it. From Vauvenargues the road continues along the north flank of the mountain until a back road allowed us to cut across the easterly slope. We returned to Aix on the D17, enjoying the vistas of the mountain that Cézanne had made so famous. He had walked the landscape with sketchbook in hand, camped and planned his next canvases on these slopes. He even maintained a cabin where he and friends could take shelter in adverse weather. In time the treks took his life, for he was caught in a rainstorm, became ill and died soon after of pleurisy.

Moustiers-Sainte-Marie is a charming village we wanted to see, so we jumped in the car on Saturday and headed up the A51, veering north-east on the D952 and passing through the small villages that were scattered across the hills.

Moustiers is built against a rock face with a great cliff rising behind it. The village is divided by a deep cut in the rocks down which waterfalls cascade. We climbed hundreds of steps to a small church at the top of the village where the view was breathtaking. On the way up we had passed a restaurant with a terrace that projects out over the falling water on the other side of the narrow gorge. Coming back down we found a small stone bridge that crossed the gorge and presented ourselves at the restaurant door.

Yes, there was a table free. Did we mind sitting outdoors? The owner showed us to the table on the very edge of the terrace. We dined in the sun while enjoying a bottle of Meursault from Burgundy and taking in the waterfalls below. Over the rooftops to the west the blue water of Lac de Sainte Croix glimmered in the distance.

The Gorges du Verdon, just a few minutes from Moustiers, is enough to unsettle a strong stomach after a full lunch. It has been described as the French equivalent to the Grand Canyon in Arizona. We drove the length of the north face, looking down to the depths to see the river far below. On the other side of the gorge and high up we could see a road cut into the steep rock wall. We returned along that south road, named the Corniche Sublime, with the cliff face on the right-hand side of the car. Marie-Hélène saw little of the vertiginous drop a few feet away as she either looked at her lap or kept her eyes shut tight, while I managed the bends in the mountain road and enjoyed the vistas.

The route down led us past Lac de Sainte Croix with specks of white sails cutting across its sparkling blue waters. Marie-Hélène's eyes were open again and she was taking in the splendid scenery.

We stopped in a village and climbed from the car to stretch our legs, and then sat on a stone wall snacking on baguette and sausage, looking over the lake.

"I'm beginning to understand this country," I said.

Marie-Hélène looked at me and then away at the lake.

"It's different and absolutely wonderful," she replied. "You didn't expect it to be the same as Canada, did you?"

By the time we returned to Aix it was after dark, and we would be leaving the following morning for Nyons.

Chapter 6

Apricots, peaches, cherries & cheeses

THE AUSTERE HIBERNATION OF WINTER had long fallen away. The *provençal* sun of mid-June changed the countryside, bringing a deeper green to the vineyards and the orchards. Strawberries began to appear in the markets, first the large, commercially grown varieties from Spain that look wonderful but lack flavour. Then a bit later come the ones from farther south in France. Finally the local varieties appear. These are smaller and harder to find, but much tastier. When the leaves are pushed aside, the strawberry patches yield their lush red berries. As the month progresses and cherries redden and apricots turn orange, trees in the orchards provide a bounty of abundance and colour.

We decided one day to take a closer look at the ripening fruit in the orchards all around us. I pumped up the bicycle tires and we started off on one of the back roads. It was an old railway line converted into a road, so the bicycling was on level ground. Then we crossed a small valley and climbed a steep section to get higher up on the hillside. A narrow lane between Venterol and Nyons winds its way through cherry and apricot orchards. The limbs of the trees sagged under the weight of the ripe fruit, and the leaves brushed our shoulders as we bicycled along. The apricots shone golden in the sun amid the green leaves. We stopped and reached up to pick a few, which we ate on the spot. Firm and luscious, their juice trickled down our fingers.

Some crops are subject to cold snaps in the spring. A year earlier there had been a late snowfall at Easter that froze the apricot blossoms on the trees, and the crop was lost. Any farmer specializing in a single crop risks losing his income for the year. Most have learned to diversify and now grow a variety of produce.

On the edge of one vineyard stood a massive lone cherry tree with its huge dome of greenery and fruit. It was so large the uppermost fruit was impossible to reach even by the farmer's longest ladder, which stood beside the tree. The ripened fruit fell, reddening the ground.

Some orchards grew apples and quince; the latter were still green and hard. Others had peach trees with oversized peaches darkening on one side. I picked one, warm from the sun, feeling its soft, velvety texture and sniffing its irresistible mouth-watering ripeness.

•   •   •

In my spare time I scoured the hillsides for more stones for the wall that had become such a challenge to me. Finding a cache that morning, I loaded them in the car, drove home, and carried them one by one to the patio. They weren't the best shape for stacking, but I was learning how to place them for stability and appearance. As the day was hot, the work progressed slowly.

I heard a familiar sound and looked up. The black motorcycle and rider came into view. However, there was something different this time. On the back and pressed against the rider was another person, clearly a woman, wearing the same style of helmet and sleek black leathers. The pair looked a bit like two identical insects, the one on the back embracing the larger one in the front. The matched leathers suggested something other than a casual friendship.

Just then Marie-Hélène drove up the road, so I walked over and opened the gate for her.

"I've bought a cherry tree at the *pépinière*. François will pick it up and plant it. Where should we put it?"

This sounded like a *fait accompli*, so I moved quickly to the next step. "Maybe there," I offered, peeling off my work gloves to point at a sunny spot.

"I was sort of thinking it should be somewhere we can see it from the patio," Marie-Hélène suggested.

"You're right. How about there?" I pointed to another spot.

"Well . . . I don't know," she said. We walked about the garden pointing at different locations until we finally agreed on one.

By the time François arrived on Friday, I had dug the hole. The tree extended off the back of his truck and had a three-foot root ball.

"Do you like it?" she asked

"It's stunning—but the hole I dug is too small," was about all I managed to say. I was distracted, looking at the clusters of ripe red cherries half hidden in the leaves.

It took both François and me to move the tree and finally set it in the bigger hole we dug. After filling soil around the roots and leaving the hose on to water it in, Marie-Hélène came out from the house with a basket in her hand.

"Will you pick some cherries for me? I want to make a *clafoutis* for dessert."

I looked at her, bemused. We had just planted the tree and now we were going to pick the cherries, all on the same day.

She sensed my wonder.

"Well, I didn't see the point in buying a tree without seeing the kind of cherries it produced," she exclaimed.

I could see François grinning. He obviously approved.

*   *   *

I was raised to believe that cheese was synonymous with cheddar. Milk could be used to make butter or cheese—that was all. However, the French, with their love of food, have taken a simple product like milk and raised it to a culinary art form.

Almost everyone in France eats cheese, and often in copious quantities. It is a superb source of protein and part of a healthy diet. Large sections of all the supermarkets are devoted to cheeses, and the weekly markets have individual artisans selling their own farm-made products.

Like wines, many cheeses are officially recognized with the French Appellation d'Origine Contrôlée status, but anyone can make cheese and sell it. And they do, from the individual fermiers to the factories of mass production. It may ripen in kitchens, or caverns deep underground, or in huge warehouses. It may be sold in its own earthenware jar or marinated in a plastic pot with grape seed oil and herbs.

Most restaurants will have a tray of cheeses from which the diner can pick and choose. The choice is so wide that no two restaurants will ever have exactly the same selection. At lunch or dinner the question is, will you have cheese or dessert—or both? One should never specify when asking for a cheese for one made

from the milk of a sheep, goat or cow. The waiter would wonder why he is bothering and may pawn off his poorest cheese on such a hapless soul. It should be referred to as *brebis, chèvre* or *vache*. Asking the names of the cheeses without a pen in hand is probably a waste of time. It is highly unlikely the diner will be familiar with all the cheeses on the tray or remember the names later anyway.

Cheeses come in every conceivable shape, size, colour and consistency. Are you in the mood for a firm cheese or a soft, runny cheese? One that was made this morning or one that is well-aged and as hard as chalk?

The rind of the cheese can take many different forms. It may have mould growing on it or no mould at all, be covered in ash or charcoal, or it may be a washed rind. The rind can be white, green, brick red or brown, and it may have herbs, pepper or chile added. Some have no rind at all; others may come wrapped in a chestnut leaf, tied with raffia.

A cheese may be a pyramid two centimetres across weighing three grams or a wheel one metre across weighing seventy kilograms. Is it sharp in flavour with blue mould running all the way through, like the famous Roquefort? Is it a *fromage frais* made yesterday? If that isn't daunting enough, then, having made a selection from the tray, the next question is—which of the hundreds of French wines is each cheese best paired with? Fortunately the server will have already made that decision and will have a suggestion in mind.

It is no wonder Général Charles de Gaulle said, perhaps at the time experiencing some exasperation with politics, "How can anyone be expected to govern a country with 325 cheeses?"

On a Thursday morning we went into the village to do our shopping. Marie-Hélène had been studying the local cheeses that turned up in the market. She had settled on a young woman who arrived every Thursday and sold *Fromage de Chèvre* from open doors at the back of her little truck. The two of them were carrying on a long conversation, so while that was going on I strayed over to a sausage merchant to buy several kinds of the ugliest-looking sausages I could find. Some, in the past, I hadn't been able to develop a taste for and gave up on, throwing them out after a week of trying. I was learning. They are made from *brebis, chèvre, vache* and *porc,* and come in all sizes, shapes and colours. I preferred the dry, chewy sausages made with nuts such as pecans, almonds or hazelnuts. I sliced them thinly, and particularly liked them with a good red wine like a Gigondas. The merchant was beginning to learn my preferences and would suggest I try certain ones.

"*Celle-ci est excellente avec un Tavel. Celle-là est très sèche,*" he said, pointing at a dark and shrivelled thing.

Marie-Hélène had finished buying her cheeses and was smiling. "I had such a nice visit with Madame Ramier. She told me how she makes her cheeses, and all the different names. Age seems to be a large part of it. She makes her *fermier* goat cheese in the traditional manner. First she explained that the milk she uses comes from her own *chèvre* cared for by herself on her own farm. She said, 'Who knows what those other *chèvre*s may have eaten?' Marie-Hélène laughed. "Talk about quality control!"

Marie-Hélène went on. "The ingredients are *'tout simples'* she says: milk, ferment and rennet to start the curdling process for cheese. On the first day the cheese is placed in little plastic containers to let the whey drain off overnight. The cheese takes on a smooth, creamy appearance and the sweet smell of goat's milk. This is known as *fromage frais.*"

I remembered Marie-Hélène ordering *fromage frais* in *bistrot*s and watching her sprinkle a little sugar on it, as is customary in Provence.

Her hands were moving. "As the cheese dries, the texture changes, becoming increasingly firm each day. So by the fourth day it is already much harder and more yellow. This is called a *'Picodon,'* which is about three inches in diameter. It develops a dry rind, and the flavour changes from very mild to something deeper and more intense."

Marie-Hélène kept on talking as we turned and began to stroll side by side through the crowded market back to the car.

"Of course I had to buy *fromage frais* as well as several older ones. Our guests will enjoy the little cheese-tasting I'm planning tonight," she announced. "Oh, I also stopped at the *fromagier* to say *'bonjour'* to Auguste. He had the most beautiful *Picodon* from Dieulefit, and a spicy *Picodon* from Grignan . . . it's a little less acidic. We can all taste it with lavender honey! Here's the *boulangerie.* Let's pick up two more baguettes. I think we're going to need them."

On the drive home, I learned that a *'fermier'* cheese is made from the farmer's own goats by the traditional method, without the same quality controls as other cheeses. It is made in the farmhouse and usually sold in the local markets. An *'artisanal'* cheese is made the same way, except that the milk may be bought from other farms. The milk for a *'coopérative'* cheese may come from a number of farms. These cheeses retain much of their regional character, and as these are generally made in larger quantities may be sold in the area or exported elsewhere. An *'industriel'* cheese is bulk production with very high standards of quality control, aimed at commercial outlets and export markets.

Chapter 7
Wine, wine, wine

THE SOURCE OF THE RHÔNE RIVER lies in the glaciers of Switzerland, where small streams rapidly become a river that cascades through the mountains of the Jura in eastern France. It turns southwest and eventually merges with the Saône River in Lyon. From there it flows southward down the fertile valley named after it, past the centres of Vienne, Tain-l'Hermitage, Valence, Montélimar, Avignon and Arles before reaching the saltwater marshes of the Camargue and emptying just west of Marseilles into the Mediterranean Sea.

The Rhône Valley is known as a gastronomic paradise that produces some of the best wines and foods in the world, and boasts the restaurants of Paul Bocuse, Léon de Lyon, Pic, and Oustaù de Baumanière, all carrying their well-earned Michelin stars for culinary excellence.

Olfactory pleasures and gustatory joys lie close to the heart of French culture, and the expression *'I sense, therefore I am'* could easily replace Descartes' famous statement *'I think, therefore I am.'* In pursuit of these pleasures, the French maintain cool underground cellars and caverns devoted to very long-term storage of their wines. Rare vintages, once consumed, will never again be tasted so they are hoarded and only brought out for special events, to be poured into fine glass chalices designed to enhance and hold the essence of the nectar. Like-minded people with keen palates seek to extract the last subtleties and complexities from a wine, comparing, learning, putting names to characteristics, categorizing, and discussing the wine like some exotic fauna being dissected on a table. Wine has developed a milieu of its own, one with a precise language to be learned and used, like a scientific discipline.

It doesn't matter that no two people will ever experience the same taste from the same wine, for no two palates are exactly alike. Searching out the characteristics in wines has become an interesting exercise in implanting a relationship in the taster's mind for him or her to find in a particular variety of grape. To suggest that 'black currant' is to be found in Cabernet Sauvignon is to attribute a characteristic to a wine. Would the connoisseur of black currants ever suggest that he finds the characteristics of a 'red wine' in his berries? The real question when the conversation has run its course remains—do you like the wine?

· · ·

To learn more about the Rhône wines, I telephoned the Université du Vin in the château at Suze-la-Rousse and made an appointment to meet the director, Jacques Mai. He met me in the cobblestone courtyard and led me into a small chapel. A sense of silence filled the space. To my astonishment, I saw that the chapel had been converted into a state-of-the-art wine-tasting room. He was justifiably proud of the facility.

In a somewhat hushed tone, he explained, "The air in the room is changed very rapidly to avoid old smells lingering during the tastings. Each cubicle is stainless steel and has running water and a sink. There is a writing surface for making notes, as well as small blinds that each taster can lower for privacy and to avoid distractions. The lighting is specially designed to show the *robe* or colour of the wine and its consistency."

As we left to walk across the courtyard toward his office, I marvelled at the brilliance of using the serene setting of a chapel for wine tasting. I looked around as Jacques led me into a large room with a massive fireplace, a desk in the centre and comfortable chairs nearby. A table in one corner was stacked with books and files, and an entire wall from floor to ceiling was lined with books on the production and consumption of wines. On another wall detailed maps showed the wine regions of France.

I asked, "Would you be able to explain to me the Appellation Contrôlée system in France?"

"*Certainement,*" he said professorially. "Appellation d'Origine Contrôlée is the French legal system for controlling and protecting the quality of wines, liquors and some dairy and farm products such as Bresse chickens, cheeses and olives. It's a clumsy name so it is simply referred to as the 'AOC'. The AOC system was created when, in the early part of the twentieth century, fraud and adulteration were damaging the reputations of these products. People were commonly making money by bringing in inferior wines from other areas and claiming it was from a quality region like Burgundy or the Rhône.

"So," he said, leaning forward and lifting one hand in a

gesture to show that something had to be done, "in 1935 the government created the Institut National des Appellations d'Origine, or INAO, allowing legal recognition of certain products from specified geographical regions so long as they met certain strict conditions such as permissible grape varieties for each region, the density of planting, pruning methods and yields per hectare. AOC profoundly changed agriculture in France and was a grand success. It also locked in a system, and whenever that is done a status quo is established and some flexibility and innovation can be lost."

That was as succinct an explanation as I had ever heard. We sat talking for the better part of the afternoon, and I learned more from him that day than from half a dozen books. When I finally left and started my drive home, I mused about Jacques Mai, a man fortunate enough to be spending his life studying wines and working in a grand château in the south of France.

The wines of the Côtes du Rhône are among the most diverse in the world. Vineyards extend down the Rhône Valley for 110 kilometres, starting at Vienne and ending at Avignon. Due to geography and climate, the valley has two distinctly different regions.

The southern Rhône wine region reaches from Montélimar to Avignon and spreads across the valley floor on both sides of the river. The best wines are the five AOC Côtes du Rhône Crus, comprised of the famous Châteauneuf du Pape, Gigondas, Vacqueyras, Lirac and Tavel. Below that are sixteen AOC Côtes du Rhône Villages wines. Then follow the AOC Côtes du Rhône Regional wines, which make up over 80 percent of the entire wines having AOC status. The *vin de pays* are considered the lowest in quality and have no formal recognition. However, nowadays that can be deceptive, for boutique wineries are appearing that make unique and outstanding wines entirely outside the AOC system. Some of these boutique wines are becoming recognized and much sought after.

The wines of the northern Rhône extend from Vienne to Valence along the steep granite hills bordering the Rhône River. There are eight AOC Côtes du Rhône Crus—Saint-Péray, Cornas, Hermitage, Crozes-Hermitage, Saint-Joseph, Condrieu, Château Grillet and Côte Rôtie. The septentrional or northern Rhône is very different from the south. The region is greener and more lush, due to the climate. The cuisine is based around products such as cattle, chickens and butter. The grape vines are predominantly Syrah for red wines, and Viognier, Roussanne, and Marsanne for white wines. It is interesting that no *rosés* are produced in the northern Rhône.

Somewhere just south of Valence, the meridional begins. It is more windswept by the mistral, drier and less green. Driving south on the A7 Autoroute du Soleil past Valence, one notices a palpable change in the clouds and the air. The broad plain of the Rhône Valley soon appears and the sun comes out. The climate demands another kind of agriculture, suitable to the arid, windier conditions of the *garrigue*, where herbs and scrub brush grow wild on the hillsides.

The words 'septentrional' and 'meridional' simply mean northern and southern respectively; however, when applied to the Rhône Valley they imply much more. They invoke the difference between two climates and all that flows from that. The southern Rhône is not as suitable for cattle, the heat is too intense and the climate too dry. Goats and sheep are more successful. Olive and fruit trees flourish. Butter is replaced with olive oil. The cuisine is lighter and often designed around Mediterranean seafood.

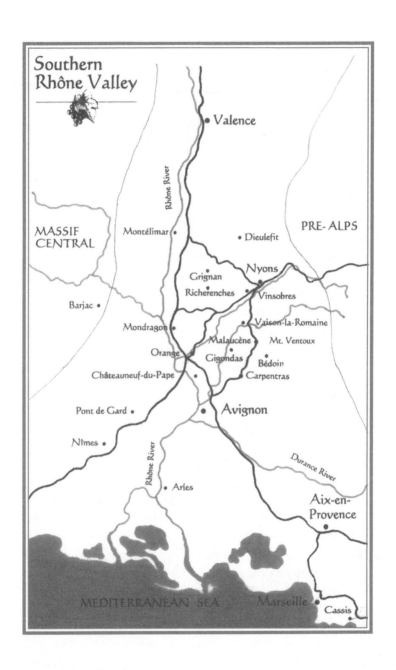

Southern
Rhône Valley

- Valence

Rhône River

MASSIF
CENTRAL

Montélimar •

- Dieulefit

PRE- ALPS

Grignan
Richérenches •

Nyons
• Vinsobres

Barjac •

Mondragon •

Orange

Malaucène •
Gigondas

Vaison-la-Romaine

Mt. Ventoux

Bédoin •
Carpentras

Châteauneuf-du-Pape •

Pont de Gard •

• Avignon

Nîmes •

Rhône River

Durance River

• Arles

Aix-en-
Provence

MEDITERRANEAN SEA

Marseille

Cassis

The wine varieties of the southern Rhône are more diverse. Of the red wines the most common varieties are Grenache, Mouvèdre, Cinsault and Carignan. The white wines are even more diverse, the major ones being Grenache Blanc, Clairette, Bourboulenc, Viognier, Roussanne, Marsanne, and the Muscat that is used to make the richly delicious dessert wines of Beaumes de Venise.

Grenache is a vine that flourishes in hot climates. It is capable of producing outstanding wines. When blended with such grapes as Mouvèdre for structure, complexity and aroma, or with Syrah, it creates the great wines of the southern Rhône. These wines can display magnificent characteristics of the *terroir*, which is the type of soil, the topography and the climate of the region. However, when too much Syrah is added to the blend, the distinctive qualities the *terroir* can bring to the wine are too easily lost, and all that is left is run-of-the-mill generic wine. Unfortunately that is what is happening, as some *vignerons* want wines that drink young without the need for aging, and the average buyer isn't interested in what the *terroir* of the valley is capable of producing.

It is only much farther north in the cooler climate and different soils of Beaujolais and Burgundy that the *terroir* is dramatically different again, this time favouring the varieties of Gamay, Pinot Noir and Chardonnay.

*   *   *

Connie and Tom Williams arrived shortly after dawn in the van they used for their cooking school. The four of us were travelling north from Nyons to the Côte d'Or in Burgundy to participate in a dinner at Château du Clos de Vougeot. Connie and Tom were from Vancouver—as we were—and had been a major influence in our decision to buy property in France. They had purchased a charming old stone *maison de village* a few years earlier that they were in the process of carefully restoring to its original style.

The A7 Autoroute took us to Valence, where we chose a route through the wine country of the northern Rhône. We crossed the Rhône River and took the N86 along the west bank through the wine appellations of Saint-Péray and Cornas before crossing back to the east bank at Tain-l'Hermitage to see the famous sun-baked slopes of Hermitage and Crozes-Hermitage. Returning to the west bank once more, we continued on N86 to Saint-Joseph and then to Condrieu and Château Grillet, which are famous for the exotic and fragrant white Viognier grape variety. The Côte Rôtie is the last northern appellation of the Rhône, producing wines from the Syrah grape as complex and fine as the great Bordeaux and Burgundies.

At Vienne we rejoined the A7 Autoroute that passes through downtown Lyon and entered a long tunnel, emerging near the southern edge of Beaujolais. This region produces on its granite soil fresh, uncomplicated and easily quaffable wines from the Gamay grape. From there we drove through the Chalonnais and the Mâconnais to our destination in the Côte d'Or of Burgundy. Considering the importance of the Côte d'Or in the world of fine wine, it is in reality a surprisingly small strip of land. The medieval city of Beaune sits at its centre.

Clos de Vougeot dates from the twelfth century and the religious order of the Cistercian monks. They enclosed the vineyard with a wall and built the château, where they made wine largely for their own consumption, until the lands were confiscated in 1790 during the French Revolution.

Today Château du Clos de Vougeot is a French historical monument entrusted to the Confrérie des Chevaliers du Tastevin.

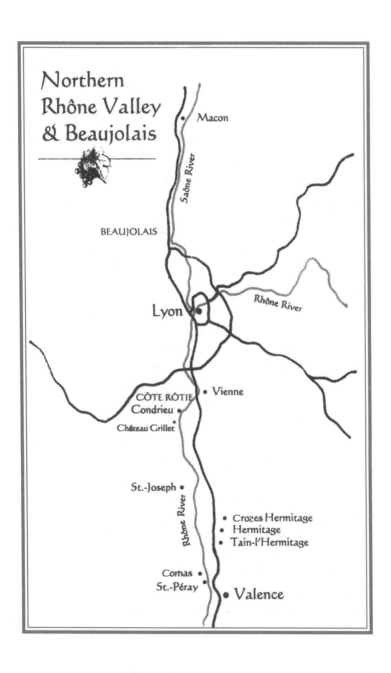

Northern
Rhône Valley
& Beaujolais

Macon

Saône River

BEAUJOLAIS

Rhône River

Lyon

CÔTE RÔTIE   Vienne
Condrieu
Château Grillet

St.-Joseph

Rhône River

Crozes Hermitage
Hermitage
Tain-l'Hermitage

Cornas
St.-Péray
Valence

The confrérie was founded during the Great Depression of the 1930s as a means of promoting the wines of Burgundy. The Second World War left the château a ruin that the Confrérie restored to its original medieval splendour in order to use as its showplace. The Confrérie expanded and in time formed commanderies around the world with over 12,000 members. Each year almost twenty dinners are held at the château for members and their guests. We were attending a June dinner called the *Chapitre d'Été*. We had spent the day wine-tasting in the cellars around Beaune and returned to our hotel to dress for a formal black-tie dinner that evening.

Cars are not permitted at the château for the dinners, so we waited for a bus to pick us up. Arriving late, we walked up the long driveway lined with empty buses toward the open gates. Entering the courtyard we were offered a *coupe de champagne*. More than 500 people from all over the world were gathered in the pleasant evening air. The ladies were stunning in spring designer gowns that looked as if they came direct from the catwalks of Paris. The gentlemen were in tuxedos, most of them bearing a silver *tastevin* hung on a crimson and gold ribbon. We had already been advised that there would likely be heads of state, royalty, academics and artists in attendance, as well as military, political and business leaders, and even astronauts.

Waiters circulated, offering canapés and more champagne. With a little effort we found our Canadian group. Then there was the sharp blare of French horns announcing that everyone was to enter the château.

The great hall is a vast *cellier* with ancient oaken beams at the ceiling supported by eight stone pillars. Long rows of tables set for the dinner filled the entire space. A number of *chevaliers* at

the head table were dressed in long gowns of crimson and gold. In front of the head table was a group of men all wearing white peasant shirts, black vests and black caps. They were the Cadets de Bourgogne, whose job it was to eat and drink with us while singing lusty drinking songs extolling the pleasures of the table and the boudoir.

A festive atmosphere filled the hall, which reverberated with animated conversation and bustling activity. Personalities were introduced and welcomed—one was a famous French actor, another the admiral of the American fleet in the Mediterranean.

The menu placed before us read *'Jamais en vain, toujours en vin,'* or 'Never in vain, always in wine.' The servers wore costumes and carried large trays held high in one hand; in the other hand were the serving implements. We began with a first course of asparagus in a Dijon and parsley sauce, accompanied by an Aligoté wine, and then moved on to a pike quenelle paired with the quintessence of white wines, Corton-Charlemagne. As far as I am concerned, Burgundy is unmatched in producing the finest and most ethereal red and white wines in the world.

Remarkably, this is done without blending, for the red variety is Pinot Noir and the white is Chardonnay.

The third plate featured poached eggs in red wine, and following that we were served fillet of duckling with morel mushrooms, paired with a marvellous Nuits-St-Georges "Les Fleurières" red wine. The wide selection of cheeses from Burgundy and elsewhere, was matched with nothing other than a Charmes-Chambertin Grand Cru.

Between courses the Cadets regaled us with song. Somewhere between the fourth and fifth courses the French horn players began playing a fanfare. The flourishes continued as they led in four men carrying a pallet held at shoulder height bearing a giant wax snail wearing a cowboy hat—thereby honouring the large American delegation present. A woman was invited to the stage. She turned out to be a *chanteuse* with a voice of pure silk. She sang a number of songs to a rapt audience and then received deafening applause to cries of *"Magnifique!" "Encore!"* When finally the hall quieted again, she was rewarded with a black cap by the Cadets and more applause.

Amid the festivities of the evening I lost track of the number of courses, however the dinner was unparalleled. I do, though, distinctly recall the desserts . . . *L'Escargot en Glace*, or snail-flavoured ice cream, followed by raspberry ice cream.

When the last plates were cleared, the servers came around with trays of small glasses containing *marc,* a clear spirit distilled from the mash left after the final pressing of the grapes for wine. A few sips of *marc* and my memory faded quickly. If nothing else was clear by then, at least the reason no cars were allowed at these dinners was perfectly obvious.

We made our way out of the courtyard and along the driveway in search of the bus we had arrived in. For me, the trip back to the hotel felt like a ride through fog on a dark London night. For some reason, late that evening what came to my mind was a statement Pliny the Elder made around 50 AD—'In Vino Veritas'—'There is truth in wine.'

Our desire for *haute cuisine* exhausted, we decided in the morning to return to Nyons by way of the slower district roads so that we could take in the countryside and the small *bistrot*s that offered simple French cooking. The food turned out to be excellent even in the most drab-looking village cafés. Invariably the café had a back section for those who wanted more than a glass of pastis and bar food. One establishment in a tiny village in the heart of the rolling hills of Beaujolais offered a freshly cooked tender pork roast with puréed potatoes, a carafe of Beaujolais and dessert. The four of us sat in that little café, sharing quiet conversation over thimble-sized cups of espresso, and feeling happy with the world.

Chapter 8

The deluge, and the old vigneron

THE SKY OVER NYONS was an intense blue in early July. We had spent most of the day gardening under the hot sun. As the afternoon progressed the heat became increasingly oppressive, and from time to time we lifted our hats to wipe our brows. The work was going well, with another area weeded and hopefully tamed for at least this season. The garden was slowly taking form, and we smiled at each other from time to time as we felt that we were becoming the masters of an area that had gone so wild from years of neglect.

In the valley to the west we began to see clouds forming and moving our way. It was an electrical storm a long way off. We stopped several times to look at it and then went on with our gardening. However, the darkening clouds continued to attract our attention. Then came distant rumbling. The black clouds had taken on a yellowish tinge, and were being lit occasionally with bolts of lightning.

We were still working in the hot sun, but straightened up as thunder resonated closer to us. Realizing our gardening was over for the day, we began to pick up the tools. . . . Of a sudden the wind came up and stirred the trees around us. Tools in hand, we headed indoors. It seemed like a good time to rest from the day of hard work; the storm would be something to watch, we thought. Then the clouds rolled into our small valley and we could see the slanting wall of rain advancing up the hillside. The wind lashed the trees and snapped at our awning over the balcony, triggering the automatic retraction system to roll it back under the eaves.

The clouds swept in much faster than we had anticipated, low over the land and brushing the hilltop. Within moments the rain was upon us, accompanied by a flash of lightning and a deafening crash of thunder that reverberated in the air. The whole sky broke into a maelstrom of forces as we dashed to close windows and doors. The deluge of falling water created streams on the hillside that rapidly turned to torrents, and we watched the road become a river. We felt engulfed in another world as successive bolts of thunder and lightning struck. Then the hail began. It made a pounding roar of its own as it moved across the vineyard next door, cutting like thousands of arrows through the greenery, turning the ground to a mixture of fallen leaves and ice. After some minutes, the sky to the west began to lighten and the sun broke through. Overhead the rain continued to fall, then abated to a sprinkle. The clouds steadily receded to the east, leaving the full arc of a rainbow over the village. The air had become fragrant and cool. The garden had changed, as the run-off had carved paths into the slope.

The whole brief event had had a theatrical feeling, I thought, as the thunder and lightning moved over the hills and into another valley. We opened the front door and stepped into the garden. The blue sky was already returning. A very wet Tabitha rushed past us on her way indoors.

The air smelled of ozone; hail crunched underfoot. We saw that the small vineyard a hundred yards up the road had had a swath cut through one side. Stripped of leaves, just the tattered bare vines remained standing. Later we found Myrtille, a veteran of this sort of weather, sleeping peacefully on our bed.

In the following days a renewed vigour became evident in the vegetation. Despite the damage caused by the hail, a spurt of new growth appeared and everything looked fresh and less stressed from the earlier heat. The bone-dry earth had absorbed the water, and the garden remained cooler and more inviting for days. The hot spell of weather was broken for a while.

•   •   •

He was standing beside the road looking at the damage to the vineyard. He must have been seventy-five years of age—a large man with a round, florid face and a stomach that created an inflated look. He wore overalls, a T-shirt and a small peaked cap that was perched slightly to one side. He also had a look of resignation on his face. Marie-Hélène and I walked over to him and introduced ourselves.

"Je m'appelle Monsieur Ladoux," he responded.

We all shook hands. He looked like a gentle man.

"C'est dommage," he said, glancing at the vineyard as if to explain what he was referring to.

"Hier nous avons eu la grêle," Marie-Hélène said, referring to the hail yesterday.

They began talking about the storm the day earlier, but his heavy patois made it difficult for me to grasp everything he said. His speech was somewhat animated and he gestured, looking back and forth, first at the vineyard and then at Marie-Hélène. I worked at understanding the conversation, but only strands of it came through. As we walked back to the house, Marie-Hélène related it to me.

"He's a very nice man. He says the loss isn't as bad as it looks because of the government subsidies. The vineyard produces just *vin de pays* and has no AOC status. There is next to no demand for it, and he either makes his own wine with it or sells the grapes to someone who can blend it with other grapes. But the interesting thing is that he owns vineyards all around the area. The Napoleonic Code requires that property be divided between the children of the owner upon death, so he would buy up plots that became too small to be usefully farmed on their own. This plot is less than half a hectare. About one-third of the crop was lost in the hail storm."

"What variety of grapes are they?" I asked.

"I didn't ask him, but you can, when you help out with the harvest in the fall."

"Yes, I thought I heard something like that," I replied.

"Well, I couldn't help but volunteer. He said he can't find workers these days and he is getting too old to do this sort of work himself. You've always expressed an interest in winemaking and I thought this was a perfect opportunity to get into a vineyard and participate. Besides, it's very colourful. You'll be able to tell all our friends that you worked in a vineyard."

I smiled at her. "Are you going to help too?"

"Maybe . . . *normalement,*" and she grinned impishly.

• • •

Our neighbour Jean Drouin, although in his seventies, was a serious and experienced hiker. When we moved into the house he saw an opportunity for companionship on his excursions. We were more than glad to oblige. With the relief of cooler weather after the recent storm, he suggested we take a lunch with us and hike up Mont Ventoux.

The third day after the storm found us driving through the village of Malaucène, which is the northern access to Mont Ventoux. Marie-Hèléne and I had driven through Malaucène a number of times. It was here that we learned that village road signs were meant for the tourists and not the locals. On approaching the village along a street lined with plane trees, we had seen a sign directing all traffic headed south to turn left. We did so and drove through the centre of the village, past all the *cafés* and *tabacs*, noticing that we were moving in an arc, until another sign directed us to turn left onto a street again lined with plane trees. After following this route several times, I wondered if the two streets were the same. The next time we approached Malaucène, I ignored the sign to turn left and drove straight ahead. Within six blocks we arrived at the other sign and had cut out the tour through the centre of the village. All the villagers knew this, but the tourists didn't, and I'm sure trade in the village had improved since the signs were installed.

Mont Ventoux, as indicated by its name, is the windy mountain. Some call it the Giant of Provence, as it reaches 1,909 metres at its barren crest. It towers over the valley, and when the mistral is blowing winds at the crest have been clocked at 320 kilometres per hour. Even after the winter snows have gone, the barren white rock on the crest looks like snow.

The mountain is accessible by road during summer months from Malaucène to the north and Bédoin to the south. It draws tourists, hikers and thousands of bicycle riders who want to test themselves against it. The Tour de France cycling race has made

Mont Ventoux famous for its steep, unrelenting climb. On the south slope we saw a plaque marking the spot where one rider burst his heart and died attempting the ascent.

After driving halfway up, Jean parked the car at the base of the ski lifts on the north flank of the mountain. From there, trails went off in three or four directions.

We took a trail that winds through the forest, at times offering glimpses of the valley. Just below the summit we broke from the trees to see parafoils fluttering like multicoloured butterflies in the air. They soared right and left but remained at roughly the same elevation on the mountainside, riding the prevailing wind from the north that collided with the mountain and rose up the slope. We continued to climb to the telecommunications tower at the summit; once there we could look down on a group of paragliders preparing to launch.

One paraglider was organizing his parafoil. First he spread it out as widely as possible on the slope, with the cords and harness extending downhill. After twisting the harness 180 degrees so that he faced uphill, he buckled it on with his back to the wind. Then, pulling on the cords and watching the parafoil fill with air, he swung round to face into the wind and ran down the slope. The foil rose sharply, lifting him off the ground and into the air.

"Oh . . . oh!" Marie-Hélène gasped.

We watched as the prevailing wind rising up the slope held him aloft. He rose higher and joined the other paragliders already riding the breeze.

One of the group split away and descended until he barely cleared the mountainside. He picked a spot to land and missed, ending up in a large shrub with the cords and foil coming down on top of him before he could scramble free.

"Ouch," Marie-Hélène said. "I wouldn't do that for any reason."

We moved on, looking for a spot for lunch. Walking over the summit and down the road on the south face, we passed a camcorder mounted on a tripod on the side of the road. There was no-one nearby. Then I saw a Japanese bicycle rider in a very dynamic cycling outfit with matching helmet struggling up the road. He rode past the camcorder, dismounted, walked back and picked it up. He carried the camcorder around the next bend in the road and set it up again. Remounting, he pedalled around the bend and past the newly positioned camcorder.

There was no wind on the south slope as we sat on a flat rock looking south over the vast Rhône Valley. The view extended to the Mediterranean to the south, across the valley to the Massif Central to the west, and east to the Alps. After lunch we put on our knapsacks and headed back over the summit. The camcorder was now on the side of the road aimed uphill, and as I looked over my shoulder I saw the Japanese rider recording his descent off the mountain.

·   ·   ·

Marie-Hélène was away on the day I made the mistake of feeling sorry for Pierre Luc. He waved from the road and I asked him if he would like to have a drink with me. His eyebrows went up and he quickly accepted, so I opened the gate and motioned him toward a garden table under an olive tree. I brought out two bottles of beer, opened them and handed one to him. Fidel had curled up under the table.

"What are you doing for work these days?" I asked straight out. The answer turned into a discursive monologue that lasted a few minutes and didn't reveal anything definite. I tried another tack.

"Pierre Luc, you have quite an orchard. What sort of apricot yield would you get each year?"

There was a shrug of his shoulders and a reflective look across the garden before his lips began to form a reply. "Well, we've had a drought for a while, the trees need some help, and besides, apricots don't sell well these days. The Turks have access to our market now and undercut our prices, so . . ." His voice trailed off without finishing the thought. He put his empty beer bottle on the table and leaned back in the chair smoking a Gauloise.

"Would you like another beer?" I asked, feeling there was more he wanted to talk about. He nodded, so I brought down two more beers. Pierre Luc talked and smoked in the same breath, tipping the ashes on the gravel patio and dropping the cigarette butts into the empty beer bottles.

The conversation moved on to more general matters like the poor condition of the French economy, largely caused by immigrant workers, and the coming municipal election where there was a chance to put a few more left-leaning people on the council. Government assistance is the lifeblood of the farmer these days.

"Do you know that there is a very good man running as a communist?" Pierre Luc asked.

I expressed my ignorance and asked, "What do you think of the far-right nationalist Le Pen?"

"Well, yes," he responded, "at least this is a man who would deal with the immigrant problem." Over more beer I learned all about the new man, Nicolas Sarkozy, and the politics of France.

By the time Pierre Luc made motions of leaving, the sun had long since set and it was approaching midnight. He had probably noticed me glance at my watch, and so he said he should be on his way. In the light of the full moon I saw him out to the gate, shook hands and then began to clear the table crowded with beer bottles. I happened to turn just as Pierre Luc was about to disappear around the bend in the road, returning to a dark and empty farmhouse.

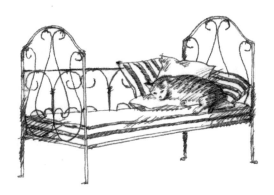

Chapter 9

Opera under the stars, and escargots in the garden

THE CHORÉGIES D'ORANGE OPERA, held since 1869, is an annual summer opera series performed in the Roman theatre in Orange, an open-air structure we had seen while shopping and touring the Roman ruins. For a theatre in a relatively remote part of the empire, a place the Romans referred to as 'the province,' they built a monument 37 metres high by 102 metres long and capable of seating 9,000 spectators. The 180-degree arc of tiered stone seating was carved out of the hillside. It is one of the few Roman theatres with its stage wall still intact, making the acoustics almost perfect.

Attempting to buy tickets for Gounod's operatic masterpiece *Romeo and Juliet*, Marie-Hélène telephoned the box office in Orange. I noticed that she had been on the phone an unusually long time when she hung up in exasperation.

"I reached the *Chorégies* ticket office and explained that I wanted to buy two tickets for the performance next Friday, and the woman said okay. So I asked if she could mail them to us and she said yes. I told her I wanted to put it on my credit card and was told she couldn't take orders over the telephone. So I asked if I could fax the request to her. She said yes, but their fax machine wasn't working that day. 'Do you have e-mail?' I asked. Yes, but she said they didn't check their e-mail very often. The best thing to do was to write to them and enclose a cheque, as they do not like credit cards. I explained that the performance was next Friday and I was concerned that they might not get the letter in time to mail us the tickets. She said, 'Don't worry, Madame, the mail works very well.'"

"So what are we going to do?" I asked, feeling some exasperation by now myself.

"Well, we can drive to Orange and buy the tickets or do what she says and mail the request with a cheque."

We decided to trust Madame's advice and mail the request. Much to our relief, the tickets arrived two days before the performance, as promised.

The balmy summer night was perfect for an opera under the stars. We had dinner on the main square and then strolled over to the theatre. The streets and restaurants were alive with the thousands of people who had come for the performance. The sidewalk in front of the theatre was crowded, everyone milling about waiting, or searching for the friends they were to meet. Slowly we worked our way into the theatre and up the hazardously steep Roman staircase. We found our seats near the top, well back from the stage, by following the numbers stencilled on the stone. I leaned backward in the hope of finding some support for my back but instead touched the legs of the woman seated behind me. She moved abruptly away and I pulled myself upright, uttering a hasty apology.

Looking around, I could see that every seat was occupied. Darkness settled in and, with a single pool of light focused on the stage, the performance began. The theatre was silent except for the music that seemed to float up to us, the bare stone stage wall holding and directing every exquisite tone and word. At the intermission we stood up, stretching our stiff backs, but there was no room to walk about. The second half of the performance began, and on the horizon we could see the flashes and hear the remote rumbling of a distant thunderstorm. It seemed to match the doomed romance building to its heart-rending dramatic climax on the stage before us.

As everyone exited the theatre, the steps on the dark stone staircase seemed even steeper and more treacherous to descend. There was only a glimmer of light coming from distant streetlights. Marie Hélène, teetering in high-heel shoes, clung tightly to my arm with both hands. As we drove home, the headlights tracking the winding roads, the words and music of the opera still ran through our heads.

• • •

By mid July Myrtille was growing healthy and blossoming under our constant attention. In fact, she was putting on weight. All the same, despite the food put down for her each day, she continued to explore and hunt. She would come and go freely, not seeking attention, but causing havoc with Tabitha. During the day she could be seen wandering in our garden or the neighbour's. Sometimes her roaming took her away for the better part of a day, and then she would show up for dinner and leave again. The warmer weather had made her more independent.

"Have you seen Myrtille today?" Marie-Hélène asked one day over dinner.

"I haven't seen her since four this morning," I said wryly, "but she'll be around by this evening." Marie-Hélène's question made me wonder as well, although I dismissed the thought and continued with my work.

By the time we turned in that night, Myrtille had not appeared. The next morning Marie-Hélène walked around the garden looking in the cat's favourite spots for napping in the shade. When she came back indoors she was a bit pensive.

"It's not like her."

"Maybe she's gone down to Yvette and Gilles'. She is their cat, after all," I offered, trying to lessen her concern.

"Should I phone them and see?" Marie-Hélène asked, looking at me to see my reaction.

"It's only been since yesterday. Let's wait a bit."

That seemed to end the matter for the time being, however by the next morning Myrtille still hadn't returned. I was becoming anxious as well, but thought it best to keep it to myself. I could already see that Marie-Hélène was on edge and not saying anything either. By dinner she was on the telephone.

"Bonjour, Yvette. Comment ça va? As-tu vu Myrtille? . . . Non? . . ."

Marie-Hélène hung up the phone after a long conversation. "She hasn't seen her for over a week. She assumed that Myrtille was with us."

We began to avoid conversation about the cat, as it simply raised our anxiety. Another day passed and I noticed Marie-Hélène walking around the garden more than usual and then along the road looking in the bushes. The walks got longer and I joined in, but we found nothing. Marie-Hélène called Suzette, who said that she had seen Tabitha sleeping in a corner of their garden, but not Myrtille.

We had already noticed that Tabitha was around the house more often, since she didn't have to contend with Myrtille.

There were daily conversations now between Marie-Hélène and Yvette about possible Myrtille sightings.

After five days, our efforts beating the bushes and calling for her had led nowhere. The situation was beginning to look bleak.

By the sixth day we had stopped searching for Myrtille. While I was washing dishes after lunch, Tabitha came up the stairs and meowed at me. She wasn't next to her food dish so I petted her on the head and went back to work. She stayed there and meowed at me again. This was a bit odd, so I looked at her and asked in French, *"Quoi?"* Why people carry on conversations with their pets I have never fully understood. I just felt it was normal.

"Meow," she replied.

She turned and walked away toward the staircase and stopped there to look at me. When I didn't move she descended a few steps and meowed again. I went over and looked at her. She meowed and walked down more steps. I followed her to the open front door where she stood waiting.

"Marie-Hélène," I hollered, "come and see this!"

Marie-Hélène arrived and we stood looking at Tabitha, who was sitting on the door sill with her back to us. She meowed once more and trotted off along the driveway to the gate.

"She's leading us somewhere," I said in a half-whisper.

"I can see that," Marie-Hélène said distractedly, but I heard curiosity in her voice.

Tabitha had by now stepped through the bars in the garden gate and was waiting on the other side. We opened the gate and she moved off again, this time across the road and toward the treed ravine on the other side. Again she stopped and waited to see if we were still following, then descended into the ravine and the trees. We struggled a bit to follow, but found her at the bottom of the ravine and ready to move up the opposite slope. A small clearing appeared, with farmer's implements scattered about and a small stone shed. Tabitha watched us approach. She just sat there. We looked around, but couldn't see anything worthy of our attention.

"She is certainly keen on something—but what?" Marie-Hélène asked.

Then we heard a weak scratching coming from the shed. I walked over and tried to throw back the rusty latch. There was more intense scratching and a croak from behind the door. I swung it open. Myrtille was standing there, a thin wraith of herself, her glossy fur now matted and unclean. She made a hoarse meowing sound, then faltered on her feet, lost balance and fell to one side.

Marie-Hélène and I froze for a split second before reacting. Together we reached inside the door to caress her. She began to purr and lay stretched out, seemingly drained of energy. Her normally loud Siamese voice could only produce hoarse mews.

"She must have been accidentally locked in here!" I said.

Marie-Hélène picked her up and cuddled her against her chest. However, Myrtille was having none of it. She refused to be held and managed to find enough energy to push herself free. Marie-Hélène acquiesced and set her gently on the ground. Myrtille walked unsteadily back to the shed and inside. We watched as she made her way around the tools and boxes to a back corner. She mewed softly. I bent over and followed. She was on a pile of rags pawing gently, and as my eyes adjusted to the dark I saw what she was after.

"There's a litter of kittens in here!" I called over my shoulder.

Marie-Hélène was now pushing her way in beside me. There appeared to be three kittens, two moving and the other one apparently sleeping.

Marie-Hélène took over. "Go get the laundry basket and a blanket. I'll stay here. Oh, bring some water too."

When I returned, Marie-Hélène was still at the back of the shed petting Myrtille and handling the kittens.

"There are three, but one is dead," she announced. "The others are very weak. Myrtille must have run out of milk. We have to get them to a vet right away."

Marie-Hélène held the basket on her knees while I drove.

The vet took one look and said, *"Très grave. Un mort, les deux autres sont faibles."*

"Et Myrtille?" Marie-Hélène asked.

"She'll be alright. She just needs *bonne nourriture maintenant.* . . . I'll check them over and give you some special food. The kittens need milk right now. I've a substitute I can give them."

Myrtille lay on the vet's examination bench and purred to her kittens. Whenever one was picked up, she complained softly and watched while the kitten was examined. She was showing concern that one was missing and wanted to find it.

An hour later we drove home to find Tabitha waiting at the front door.

Marie-Hélène was on the telephone. *"Yvette, nous avons retrouvé Myrtille! Elle a une litière de chatons!* Come over!"

The laundry basket was lined with an old blanket and converted into a secure nest in the corner of our bedroom. We took turns watching the kittens and comforting Myrtille. Tabitha was there, curious and watchful. She slept on the corner of our bed, and from there she could keep an eye on the new family.

It was agreed that Myrtille and her new family would stay at our house for now. The kittens would be a bit older when we left in the fall, and they could then all move to Yvette and Gilles' home.

•   •   •

Marie-Hélène and François were examining the new rose bushes.

"Those things!" exclaimed Marie-Hélène as François picked up several snails and moved them. "How do I get rid of them?"

François looked at her, "They're good. Don't you like *escargots?*"

"They're awful. They eat the leaves off my plants."

I was gardening nearby so I could overhear parts of their conversation. François spent some time discussing the subject. It seems that *escargots* are protected by law and can't be harvested until the reproductive season is over.

Since no one eats an escargot that hasn't been cleaned out, several ways have been developed to purge their systems. Some starve the *escargots* for several days, giving them lots of water, while others think feeding them oatmeal is best. François expressed his preference for feeding them fresh dill to purge their systems faster, keeping them in a wood box with holes in the bottom for good ventilation.

"Once that is done we freeze them. They keep quite a long time. The stores even sell flavoured butters just for *escargots,*" he said. Marie-Hélène listened with fascination while studying the damage to her rose bushes.

I spent part of the day placing my recently acquired stones on the beginnings of the wall. When I ran out of stones I went indoors to see Albin and his workers laying the last floor tiles in the guest suite. When they had left for the day, I walked over to see what François and Marie-Hélène were finishing up in the garden.

"François, would you like a drink?" We were all dehydrated from the work, so sitting down in a shady corner with glasses of Orangina was a refreshing way to end the day. It was also a chance to chat.

"Would you like to come to our house for dinner next Sunday?" François asked.

"Of course we would," Marie-Hélène responded.

Sunday arrived and we put on dressier clothing. We felt it was an honour to be invited to François and Manon's home.

Their village, situated on a high and remote hillside well into the Pre-Alps, consisted of fewer than thirty houses and a church that seemed large considering the size of the village. Manon described being raised there and how her bedroom was suspended between two houses over a narrow road. The road happened to be the access to the village and when trucks began to come up the hill they couldn't pass beneath, so the bedroom had to be taken down.

Despite the elevation, there was a spring that ran year-round, supplying drinking water. Without it the village would not have existed.

The four of us slowly walked the village together, talking about its history, and then returned to their house for dinner. The first course was a truffled omelet, which announced itself with a pungent, earthy aroma. When the plates from this course were gathered up, François came out of the kitchen with a mischievous smile spread across his face, carrying two very hot plates judging by the thick kitchen gloves he was wearing. He set down before each of us a dozen *escargots*. The main course was *escargots!*

Marie-Hélène gasped and said, *"Oh, mon dieu!"*

François was beaming with pleasure.

The *escargots* were just out of the oven, piping hot and bubbling in garlic butter. The flavour was superb, and when François saw that we were delighted and had finished the plates he went into the kitchen and returned with another dozen for each of us.

"We harvest and freeze them every fall," he explained.

My curiosity aroused, I asked how many they had.

"Thousands," he replied. "Enough to get us through until next year."

Chapter 10
Early life in Provence

LIVING IN PROVENCE was one thing, but to understand the way of life I had to read some of the literature, so I stopped by the bookstore in the village. The *'librairie,'* as it is called, offered all the great French classics as well as books on truffles, mushrooms that were safe to eat, and the usual assortment of travel guides. I noticed a window display featuring René Barjavel, an author from Nyons. Then, at the next Thursday outdoor market, I stopped at the used book stall and noticed a title that read:

BARJAVEL
La charrette bleue

Picking up the tattered copy, I read the back cover. This was an autobiography—his childhood memoirs of growing up over a *boulangerie* on Rue Gambetta—describing life in Nyons in the early 1900s and the lives of the peasants and artisans who subsisted with their hands and tools. I knew Rue Gambetta and the bakery—it still bears his name. His mother was raised in a house two hundred yards from ours. The name on the mailbox is Achard, her maiden name. I was hooked.

Barjavel transformed my view of Nyons by introducing me to a way of life that has almost entirely vanished.

The houses were built from the stones dug out of the fields. Oil lanterns lit the rooms at night. Women wore ankle-length dresses. Sheep often filled the streets as the herders moved their flocks between grazing fields. Goats, kept for milk and *chèvre* cheeses, commonly occupied the ground floor of the house. Cattle were rare as they ate and drank too much, and did not thrive in the hot southern climate. A man with his mule weighed down by tools would arrive once a year and set up in the square, where he relined copper pots and pans with molten tin. The landscape was arid and water hard to come by. A spring on a farm meant there was water to drink, to cook and wash with. If the source dried up, farmers dug caverns hoping to gather the moisture that condensed on the ceiling drop by drop. Milk and wine were safer to drink than well water. Streets of the village were narrow and oriented north to south to provide shade from the intense summer sun. I learned that snow was likely each winter and that summer thunderstorms created flash floods in the Eygues River that runs through the village.

Barjavel's grandfather came from the village of Tarendol, in a desolate area of marginal farmland. He grew "a little hard, dry wheat" and harvested almonds from the few trees that survived in the harsh climate. Returning exhausted from his work, he would wind his hand into the tail of his mule and let the mule guide him home as he slept walking behind. When the mule reached the haystack in the yard and stopped, he woke, climbed the stone stairs to his house, opened a small cupboard where he kept his meagre supply of food, and ate a tiny bit of chocolate before going to bed. He heard that a *boulanger* in Nyons was looking for an apprentice, so before dawn the following day he and his thirteen-year-old son set off to walk for five or six hours the thirty kilometres to Nyons. The son was hired, so the father returned alone to Tarendol the same day.

A baker's life held an inherent health risk. The very flour used for baking clogged the lungs. Barjavel's mother was married at seventeen and widowed at twenty-five when her first husband died of the baker's pulmonary disease. In time the young apprentice would become her second husband and Barjavel's father.

Lavender grew wild, and the men organized the women and children to cut and gather it all day, bent over in the full sun. Poisonous snakes would hide in the shade of the rocks and herbs and strike at the bare legs of the workers. Despite the hard work, they sang while they worked, whether in their homes or outdoors in the fields. Each family had a precious notebook of songs in a drawer. René's father was conscripted for the First World War and was away for years, as were most able men. Many did not return home. The farms and businesses were run by the women, who would gather at the railway station when the train came in to see if their man or their son was on board. Barjavel related the story of a woman whose husband had been killed in the war and had received no news from her son in a month. Dressed in black she came each day to stand at the back of the station, waiting for the train to arrive.

Nyons was a railway terminus, so soldiers were stationed there. When the soldiers heard they were to be sent to the front, they drank too much alcohol in the bars and roamed the narrow streets. Barjavel recalled playing in the street when his mother saw a group of drunken, rowdy soldiers approaching. She picked him up, ran indoors and closed the shutters. One soldier drove his bayonet into the shutter.

His father was away three years, returning in 1919 when Barjavel was eight years of age. They didn't know each other.

Barjavel's mother never left Nyons. He, on the other hand, was a bright boy and left to pursue his education. As a journalist and author, he settled in Paris. When he returned in middle age for a visit with his own children, he showed them the bayonet scar in the shutter. I went to investigate for myself and, yes, ninety years later it was still there.

•   •   •

The very things that made Provence an irrelevant rural backwater on the world stage in time came to be the reasons people were attracted to it. The constant sunshine, the dry climate, the escape from the urban rush, and the way of life grew on everyone who visited. In time the depressed real estate became valued and then sought after. *Provençal* country furniture became *'à la mode.'*

Stone ruins were considered charming and were even looked on as an opportunity.

Then the writers arrived and portrayed the region as colourful, with a wonderful way of life. That in its way completed the cycle and made Provence an event in itself. It became a destination. It was 'in' to spend one's vacation in an old farmhouse and to bicycle on the winding back roads amid the vineyards. The people of Provence loved the attention because they already knew how agreeable life was in the rolling farmland. To see others recognize this was flattering. Furthermore, the attention brought money. It was good to receive government subsidies, but the money from tourism was even better. It brought a new affluence. Yesterday's ruin was today's château, and a piece of old used furniture was viewed as a valued treasure. To say something was 'provincial' no longer meant it was backward and unappealing. Provence took on cachet. It had been discovered.

· · ·

As beautiful and hospitable as the climate is, the people who lived in Provence struggled to earn a living in a region emerging from the poverty Barjavel describes. Each village therefore sought out a unique event that would draw visitors. Dieulefit has become a pottery centre. Richerenches started a flower festival. L'Isle-sur-la-Sorgue grew into the second-largest antique market in France. Bédoin and Malaucène draw thousands of cyclists each year, as they are situated at the base of Mont Ventoux.

The farmers, not to be outdone, came up with a *ferme en ferme,* a weekend in which they open their farms to visitors. At first a few vegetable farmers, winemakers, cheese makers and potters attracted some visitors to their farms and studios. As the event's success grew, more farmers and artisans participated.

A brochure with a map is now published, announcing the weekend and the participating farms and studios.

Starting out early on Saturday morning, we passed the entire day driving between the *fermes* tasting, sampling and buying. At one farm, the lady made *chèvre* cheeses in her kitchen, the plastic mesh cups draining off the excess moisture. Children visiting from the cities petted the heads of the goats and sheep. At another, dyed mohair throws and scarves of all colours were for sale. The male, or buck, goat was stretched out on a clean blanket in the sun. Its long, smooth, shiny fleece was well-combed for this day. I asked the owner how often the buck was sheared and was told just twice a year. The fleece had to be long to make the best mohair. We bought a throw in a sky blue colour.

A potter opened his *atelier* to show how he made pottery, from the throwing of the clay on a spinning wheel to glazing the pieces for colour and finish, to firing them in a kiln. For the *vignerons*, all the problems of having a stranger knocking on a busy farmer's door and asking for a personal tour or tasting were avoided. The range of farms expanded to include orchards, jam and jelly makers and even *escargot* farms. *Ferme en ferme* became so successful that long lines of vehicles in the driveways of the farms came to be expected. The festive and welcoming atmosphere drew even more visitors.

As people flowed into their normally tranquil surroundings, the restaurant owners geared up for these special weekend events, with the entire family turning out to help cook, serve and, of course, bring the tab the moment a patron caught the eye of the server. With the new activities everyone prospered.

•   •   •

Sunday has taken on an importance in Provence as a day when some special leisure activity should take place. The old pious tradition of a day of rest has been replaced by the notion of a day of pleasure. On the roads just before noon, drivers are seen rushing impatiently to a restaurant or to friends' homes for an appointed lunch. The traffic is intense. Then, just after noon it vanishes, leaving the roads nearly empty for hours. All the people dashing about in their cars have arrived at their destinations, and Sunday lunch is underway. A reservation is essential as the restaurants are crowded.

Sunday is the day that the cycling teams of identically outfitted *véloistes* race along the roads. A queue of vehicles lines up behind, waiting for a chance to pass. Then there are the grandfather/grandson teams, again in identical outfits, riding side by side. The drivers don't seem to mind. A horn is never blown in frustration; after all, the next weekend it may be their turn. Finally, there are the friendly groups of husbands and wives or companions generally dressed *sportif* and out for a bike ride to the next village, where the restaurant owner has set aside a table on a shaded patio just for them. I have always admired how after a long lunch enjoyed with copious amounts of wine they manage to pedal home.

Motorcycles appear as well. Sleek, high-powered bikes in groups of three or four riders or even a dozen wind their way at high velocity along the best mountain roads, passing the cars with bursts of speed and quick swerves across the centre line. They look like they have been riding all weekend and at those speeds it is impossible to tell how far they have travelled.

If a row of motorcycles or *vélos* is parked in front of a restaurant, those arriving late know that lunch will be running behind. At that point it may be best to look for another restaurant, or simply relax and enjoy the afternoon.

A dress code is no longer *de rigueur*, unless possibly along generational lines. The older diners still put on their smart clothes while the younger ones wear T-shirts and jeans. We tried a restaurant on a back street of Vaison-la-Romaine. The atmosphere was charming and its clientele were obviously the villagers. At one large table, a family gathering was well underway when we arrived. People of all ages seemed to be enjoying the chance to see each other, possibly because they hadn't been together for some weeks.

An elderly couple entered the restaurant, graciously shaking hands with the owner. The owner, in turn, warmly acknowledged them, and with a flourish of his hand led them to a waiting table. The gentleman was wearing a smart autumn-tone sports jacket, wool slacks, dress shoes and the obligatory Hermès tie. His wife wore a Parisian suit, which was possibly a bit tighter fitting than when it was purchased, and conservative high-heeled shoes.

They each ordered a half-bottle of wine; he preferred red and she preferred white. The first glass was poured and was nursed through the appetizer course. The second glass was for the main course, after which they leaned back and, seemingly with all the time in the day ahead of them, sipped the wine while continuing their conversation. The waiter understood that until the wine glasses were eventually empty he was not to return to their table. At the right moment he arrived with dessert menus. The leisurely pace continued through dessert and then two espressos. The pleasure and style they enjoyed on that day seemed much keener than that of the other diners. Sunday lunch could be a special event worth dressing for and enjoying fully.

On the drive home, Marie-Hélène began to talk about the cultural differences between Canada and France. "For instance, restaurants are rarely noisy here. Guests speak quietly so as not to be overheard or interfere with other tables. In Vancouver, restaurant owners seem to fear quiet and immediately turn up the music far too loud. They could take a lesson from the French."

Just then we passed a man standing at the side of the road with his car door open. He was facing the ditch and studying the sky with a look of relief on his face.

"Yuck," Marie-Hélène said as she looked away.

*   *   *

I had driven to the *tabac presse* in Nyons early and returned with the *Herald Tribune* and fresh-baked croissants. Marie-Hélène had made coffee. She picked up the paper I had laid on the kitchen table and began reading.

"There's an article in the *Trib* about Châteauneuf-du-Pape.

115

I didn't know it's the most famous wine in the southern Rhône. He describes it as 'earthy and sometimes fierce, the proverbial "brooding" wine.' Here we are in Provence, in the Rhône Valley, and we haven't even *been* there. Let's go—we've got the day free. Châteauneuf is between Orange and Avignon, less than an hour away."

I was pouring coffee as she continued. "He calls it 'a land of blends.' The AOC rules permit the use of up to *thirteen* varieties of grapes in the wine, and one château actually uses all thirteen. Boy, is that different from Burgundy, where there's no blending allowed."

Before we started out, Marie-Hélène pulled some wine books off the shelf and carried them to the car.

Once on the road she began to read. "Here's some information. Châteauneuf receives 2,800 hours of sunshine each year. The AOC system actually started there in 1923 and was so successful that it spread across France. The village is situated on a knoll with the ruins of the château at the top."

She paused to read more. . . . "This is interesting—the château was the summer residence of the popes, who built it to escape the noise and problems of Avignon in the fourteenth century. That sounds like Avignon today! They apparently picked the knoll for its outstanding panoramic view of the rolling hills."

Marie-Hélène fell silent reading again. . . . "Apparently the village has been fully restored and is a tourist destination, with wine caves and shops on its narrow, winding streets. Châteauneuf-du-Pape literally means 'the new residence of the pope.' It was destroyed by fire during the religious wars and then blown up in 1944, so it's just a ruin today."

We parked in the village at the base of the knoll and walked up a wide staircase to the château to see the view of vineyards stretching almost to the horizon. Then, turning to walk back down, we found just below the ruins a restaurant and wine cellar in the Verger des Papes, where the popes had had their orchard. We stopped to see the view from the huge terrace of the restaurant overlooking the sun-drenched distant green vineyards. There was an Eden-like quality to the settling.

"After we've seen the cave, I'd like to have lunch here," I said.

Marie-Hélène just nodded as she turned her head, taking in the view. "It's beautiful."

The cave was just what you'd imagine a cave to be. A set of tunnels had been dug out of the hard soil. The ceiling and walls dripped moisture. Wine bottles had been affixed to the walls by metal hooks for display. The uneven floor had cases of wines scattered in a haphazard manner so that visitors had to step around them.

"*Bonjour!*" a man hollered from one of the tunnels when we entered.

"*Bonjour,*" I replied.

He immediately switched to English as he walked toward us with his hand extended. "My name is Pierre Delon. Can I help you?"

Pierre turned out to be multilingual. He had travelled the world learning about wines and had even spent time in the Sonoma Valley in California.

I got to the point. "We'd like a primer on what Châteauneuf wines are all about."

"Okay," he said and started in.

Although all thirteen grape varieties can be used, in fact the winemakers are free to blend in any proportions they choose. The dominant grapes are Grenache Noir, Mouvèdre and Syrah. Of course with that kind of choice Châteauneuf wines can be very different and generally fall into groups. All the winemakers will blend to bring out the characteristics they want in their own wines.

Pierre opened a bottle and poured some wine into three glasses. "Taste this one. It's predominantly made from Grenache Noir, a sweet, almost jammy variety when fully ripe. It brings to the wine lush raspberry and currant flavours."

We all sipped the wine, and Marie-Hélène said, "I get a dried herb aroma."

"That's very perceptive," Pierre responded. "Few people pick that up.

"Now, by contrast, taste this one," he said, pouring another wine. "This winemaker uses much more Mouvèdre, and you should be able to find a firmer structure, meatiness and elegance in the wine. It's a bit young, and the tannin will bite the top of the tongue."

We tasted this wine while Pierre poured a third in another set of glasses. "This one has a lot of Syrah, the red that is used almost exclusively in the northern Rhône. It brings a darker colour to the wine." We looked at the colour and then breathed in the round and full fruity aroma before tasting the wine.

"In the southern Rhône soil, Syrah can be a bit flabby and lacking in structure, but when blended it adds warmth and strong accents of plums, black cherries and spice.

"Think about those massive Australian Shiraz wines. That's just this Syrah grown in different conditions."

I was curious. "Does any winemaker use all thirteen varieties?"

"Yes, Château Beaucastel does. They make one of the best wines in Châteauneuf, but in their own style. It's meant to age ten to fifteen years before drinking. At first it's somewhat hard and closed, but in time it opens, revealing layers of fruit backed up by firm structure."

He hesitated. "Are you having lunch upstairs?"

"Yes we are—on the terrace."

"Good. I recommend you order a Beaucastel and I'll ask the waiter to bring you one of the better old vintages that's not shown on the wine list. It pairs magnificently with roast beef, game or *coq au vin*. For cheeses you should try the Roquefort and St. Marcellin."

Following the recommendations from Pierre we were treated to an extraordinary lunch. I chose the roast beef and Marie-Hélène the *coq au vin*. The wine turned out to be a '95 vintage. The waiter decanted it very slowly and carefully at our table so as not to disturb the heavy layer of sediment in the bottle. He then poured a small amount into my glass for me to taste. Even before lifting the glass I could smell the earthiness of the wine. As I raised the glass to my nose, deep, smoke-like scents laced with cherry and raspberry drifted through my nasal passages. Then other qualities began to emerge. The wine had layers of dried herbs and spices. The firm structure from the Mouvèdre seemed to give the wine cohesion, so that no matter how the scent and taste shifted as we consumed it with the food, it held its character and stood up to complement the strong flavours of our dishes. With the sharp Roquefort a grand harmony was reached.

We bought seven cases of wine: two of each style we had tasted and one of Beaucastel. After lunch I drove the car up the hill and Pierre helped us load the cases in the trunk. Our ever-growing wine cellar took on another dimension that day.

Chapter 11
No guests please, Beth

WE HAD MADE A STANDING RULE for this summer—no guests unless it was absolutely unavoidable. The plan was to devote our time to the completion of the guest suite and to the garden.

It was near the end of July and Marie-Hélène was on the telephone for a long time. The conversation seemed one-sided, with Marie-Hélène doing all the listening and only asking a question now and then.

"Beth is coming to stay for a week," she said upon hanging up.

"Oh," I responded, leaving room to hear more.

"She and her husband are separating and she's distraught. Apparently she booked a flight to France to get away and was just going to travel for a while. Then she remembered that we were here and called to say she would be in Avignon on Thursday. I *couldn't* just say no, could I?"

I heard the concern in her voice. "Of course you could," I teased.

"Oh, shut up," she rallied back.

"Well, it shouldn't make much difference, since we'll be here anyway. Let's just be clear that we're working and don't have time for touring."

Thursday came and we headed toward Avignon. We had learned that some of the drivers in Provence show no fear. A slow driver was evidently someone travelling at ten kilometres per hour above the posted speed limit. The narrow, winding roads have no shoulders, and deep ditches on both sides leave no margin for error. Few opportunities exist to pass the slower drivers.

Why the drivers in Provence are so aggressive is a mystery to me, for in the rest of France they are far more rational. To say that it is cultural doesn't properly account for the madness. The drivers exhibit little sense of risk analysis, such as passing while going into blind corners. It is as if they have decided there is no vehicle coming until they can actually see it. The local newspapers regularly report deaths on the roads and the locations. We had driven by several of these and could see skid marks of tires stopping abruptly in the middle of the road, or veering off into the ditch. The reporting of the carnage didn't seem to change the attitudes of the drivers.

We were between Nyons and Malaucène when an example of the typical driver presented itself. I was following a truck when a car appeared in my rear-view mirror, approaching fast. He couldn't pass, so instead he just came up as close as physically possible behind our car and stayed there. We soon came around a bend in the road and he took his opportunity, pulling out quickly and accelerating to get by us. Then I saw another truck coming toward us around a bend in the road ahead. But the driver who had now passed us didn't pull in ahead of us.

Instead he accelerated even more, in an attempt to pass the truck as well. I gritted my teeth and braked. Marie-Hélène reached out and braced herself against the dashboard.

The gap closed between the vehicles and the trucks moved to the far edges of the road while braking hard, but it was too late. The car tried to squeeze down the middle, unsuccessfully. First it scraped against the truck ahead and then bounced over a few inches and collided with the truck coming toward us. The car spun around and wound up in the ditch. The trucks came to a stop, and the drivers were getting out. We crept forward and between them.

"Aren't you going to stop?" Marie-Hélène asked.

"No. No way," I insisted. "We have to be at the train station in Avignon in half an hour, and I'm not getting caught up in police reports and investigations by the *gendarmerie* at this point."

We kept on moving.

As we approached the outskirts of Avignon, Marie-Hélène said, "By the way, you should know that Beth is very conversational."

"Are you saying that she talks a lot?"

"Well . . . yes, you could say that. I thought you should know," she said, glancing over at me.

Beth was standing on the TGV platform when we saw her. She looked small with the two oversized suitcases on either side of her. After many hugs and kisses, Marie-Hélène and Beth walked down the platform, leaving me to follow with the suitcases in tow.

One case barely fitted into the back of our rental car and the other slid into the rear seat next to Beth.

"The flight was dreadful. The man next to me wanted to talk all the time and tried to pick me up. I couldn't find the TGV station at Charles de Gaulle Airport. Nobody would help me, and I had to push a cart with my luggage I don't know how far. At the train station where I was buying my ticket, the woman snapped at me, 'Speak English, please!' I thought my French was quite good."

She leaned forward and tapped Marie-Hélène on the shoulder in a meaningful way before continuing. "Then I almost missed the train, but a very helpful train attendant told me where to stand and wait. I managed to get one bag on the train and the door started to close. I had to have someone hold the door while a nice man lifted the other bag on board for me. That train moved so fast I could hardly see the countryside. But I'm here, and it's so good to see you two."

As I parked the car in our driveway, Beth was winding up her marital monologue. "I will have to go on with my life in some other place, away from all that."

Marie-Hélène changed the subject. "Can I show you the room we made up for you?"

I carried in one suitcase and set it down in the extra room. The hide-a-bed had been opened and neatly made up with fresh linen. Towels were folded on a chair.

"Oh, it's so quaint. Where do I hang my clothes?"

Marie-Hélène helped Beth while I went to get the other suitcase from the car.

The next morning after the breakfast that Marie-Hélène had prepared and while I cleaned up the dishes, Beth asked, "Well, what is there to do today?"

Marie-Hélène was ready. "Well, Gordon is working with the gardener and keeping an eye on the mason's progress. I have to strip wallpaper. Why don't you walk down to the village and look around?"

"Good idea! I'd like to see some French boutiques," she said.

As it turned out, Beth spent the morning unpacking as best she could and only reappeared near lunchtime. She and Marie-Hélène kept up a steady conversation, so I ate quickly and headed back to the garden.

Jet lag caught up with Beth and she turned in early that evening. When we were settled in bed, Marie-Hélène said, "You know, I couldn't get her to stop talking about her problems, so finally I said the wallpaper was taking me longer to strip than I had thought, and offered to show my problem to her. She looked at it and only said that she'd better let me get back to work!"

Beth didn't resurface until almost noon the next day. "I saw that you both were working, so I made something to eat so as not to bother you. Is that okay?" she wondered.

"That's great, Beth," Marie-Hélène answered, washing up to prepare lunch. "Would you like some lunch?"

"Oh, no. I've had enough, thanks."

The conversation veered to her separation problems, and I could see Marie-Hélène was learning the many details. I began to realize that every conversation was going to be about her marital troubles.

*　　*　　*

Fields of olive trees with their gnarled trunks and silvery leaves that glistened against the blue sky grow everywhere in this region. Our garden had eleven mature olive trees, although in sorry, neglected condition. It occurred to us that these trees could produce our own olives. It would take some work, though—at least on the part of François, as we didn't know anything about olive production. After being consulted the first summer we owned the property, he walked the garden with the manner of a doctor examining a patient. He inspected each tree, one hand on his chin, the other handling the bark and leaves. The serious concentration on his face had me convinced that the trees were beyond recovery and might have to be uprooted and replaced. When he finished and walked over to us, he described several diseases that needed to be dealt with, as well as a root problem. As bad as he said it was, all the same within a couple of years of his careful attention our trees would improve and once again yield an abundance of olives.

When François returned the next Friday, he brought a load of soil that he mounded around the base of each tree. Then he appeared a week later and put on a suit and face mask that looked like an early design by NASA. Getting out a large tank of chemicals, he hoisted it onto his back and suggested to us that we should close all the windows and shutters and either stay indoors or go somewhere else for a few hours. We stayed inside and watched as he turned the air blue with chemicals. The trees remained that colour for weeks. He sprayed the trees twice that summer. The next year the leaves were greener, the olives more abundant and larger. I never tried to calculate the cost per olive, but they were *our* olives, so it didn't matter. It also didn't matter that we wouldn't be there in December to harvest the crop.

We had learned that Nyons was famous for olives, as it was the first olive-growing area in France to receive an Appellation d'Origine Contrôlée designation for quality. This is an important seal of approval and helps to control the quality and raise the price of the product, just as it has done for the wine industry. In the winter of 1956 the temperature fell to -20 °C and half the olive trees were lost. By 1994 the recovery was so strong that the Institut National des Appellations d'Origine Contrôlée granted their coveted status to Nyons. All qualifying olives and olive oil bear on their containers the designation 'AOC Nyons.'

Not knowing much about this treasure, we began buying and tasting the olives and olive oil from the *Coopérative Agricole de Nyons*. The crushed olives make a tapenade spread that is delicious with an apéritif. And after noticing that many local homeowners had given their properties a name, we named our property *'Les Oliviers',* after our trees.

Olives are harvested in a number of ways: shaking the branches, hitting them with sticks and combing them with rakes made expressly for the purpose. The olives fall on nets spread under the trees. The *coopérative* is a modern commercial enterprise with stainless steel tanks and centrifuges. However, Nyons has two museums showing olive *moulins* dating from the eighteenth century. One is across the road from the *coopérative* and the other is on the dyke next to the fourteenth-century arched stone bridge. Of course there is a confrérie for olives in Nyons.

François told us, "Your trees are *tanche oliviers*. The variety is unique to this area. The olives are black and plump with a rich, meaty texture. They're less bitter than other varieties, and have a nutty taste."

The *tanche* is locally called the *'olive noire.'* AOC Nyons production comprises about 400 tons of olives and 200 tons of olive oil. This compares to French production of 2,000 tons of olives and 2,500 tons of olive oil. Most of the Nyons product is consumed in the region, with little ever shipped abroad, partly due to the small production and partly due to the price it commands.

What makes AOC Nyons olives so unique is the climate, the soil, the rarity of the *tanche* variety and the method of preparation. The olives are picked in December or January and immersed in ten-per-cent salt brine for six months, to permit the acid in the fruit to dissipate. They take on a dark maroon colour, like that of a monk's robe.

The *Coopérative Agricole du Nyons* in its promotional material describes its olives as being rich in vitamins and carotene, and providing more energy than other fruits or vegetables. One seller goes so far as to say, "Whoever eats olives every day of every season will become as old and strong as the beams of a very solid house."

The olive oil is made by cold pressing the fruit. From 100 kg of olives, about 20 to 25 kg of extra virgin olive oil is produced, as well as 20 to 25 kg of water and 50 kg of pulp. The oil is pure juice without any chemicals or preservatives added. The result is an unctuous, fine and fruity oil with a green-gold colour. It has aromas of green apple, fresh herbs and almonds.

Olive oil is the cornerstone of cooking in the south of France and throughout the Mediterranean, just as butter is in the north. However, the oil produces a lighter cuisine that is easier on the waistline and reputedly helps fight cancer and heart disease. Some consider it one of the oldest known sources of food.

Tapenade is made by removing the pits and crushing the fruit. It may be pure or have herbs and capers added. Another recipe uses green olives and anchovies. Tapenade is eaten on toast, like caviar, or as a condiment in place of mustard for cold meats, sauces, and in omelets.

With olives, nothing is wasted. The pulp is returned to the orchards for fertilizer; the pits are refined into olive seed oil.

We began to shop at the *coopérative* regularly, as they sell wine by the bottle or by the kilo. There is a scale in one corner of the store and what looks like four gas pumps next to it. The *Nyonsais* arrive with their own containers, place them on the scale and fill them from a hose with white, *rosé*, or a choice between two qualities of red wine. One day I watched a man carry in a twenty-litre plastic container and fill it to the brim. I wondered if he had a large family, but his florid complexion told another story. We restricted our bulk purchases to a litre of white and a litre of *rosé* at any one time. The red was so young it tasted like a wad of cotton on the tongue. It needed a lot more time on its own for the tannins to soften.

The second fall we owned the house, when we were preparing to leave for Canada our first significant crop of olives was ripening. It would need picking in December during our absence, so we offered the crop to Jean and Suzette if they wanted to pick them. They were delighted. We felt it was the least we could do considering the extraordinary dinners they had prepared for us at their home.

Returning this spring, we were once more invited over. We had already learned that these dinners were an all-evening event, starting with apéritifs and hors-d'oeuvres and then moving to the dinner table for three full courses. This time Suzette served a truffled omelet and a wild boar daube. Each course was generously followed with offers of second helpings of everything. The boar turned out to be surprisingly similar to beef, but richer and deeper in flavour. Jean treated us to bottles of old wines from his cellar. He carried them upstairs in a towel and wiped the caked-on dust from the bottles before setting them on the table. The labels were stained and hard to read. One that I managed to make out told me that we were drinking a twenty-two-year-old Châteauneuf-du-Pape. It was wonderfully mellow and elegant on the palate.

Jean and Suzette Drouin had owned the best *pâtisserie* in Nyons before they retired. Having dessert in France is considered normal and the quality is generally high. However, their desserts simply surpassed all others, and were inevitably accompanied by a *digestif.*

When it was time to leave, Jean brought out a bag containing four jars of preserved olives and two litres of olive oil. He said this was our share of the olives they had picked.

"Pour nous? Nos olives! Vous êtes trop généreux!" Marie-Hélène enthused. With great pride we carried our own olives and olive oil home, and tasted both before turning in for the night. The renowned nutty quality of the *tanche* was definitely there.

Another subject that came up during dinner that evening had left Marie-Hélène and I thinking about the changes taking place in rural France. Suzette had said that their son refused to take over the *pâtisserie* when she and Jean wanted to retire. He moved to Australia, where he became a chef. So the *pâtisserie* was sold. It was not unusual for many of the youth to move away from their villages. The isolated rural areas did not offer a lot of opportunity for young people. Many wanted to escape to bigger centres, where their livelihood not so tied to the land.

Even though two major winter freezes had killed the olive trees to the ground and years of crops were lost, olive trees are so hardy that the roots survived and the trees grew back. The loss of the men in two wars made many farms and businesses unviable and almost brought about the collapse of the traditional way of life. The sons and daughters who remained at home faced a new way of life. They still lived by the old farm or business unit of their parents struggling to make a living, but the patriarchal family structure had been weakened. Without the men and with just the women to run them, the farms and small businesses were less self-sufficient. If there was no family farm or business to take over from their parents, the youth had to take whatever employment was available. Most of it was dull, repetitive work. It was mind-numbing and stifling to the eager hopefulness of youth.

During the worst decades some villages were actually abandoned and left to crumble. The only thing that saved others was the outside money of city people who liked the warmer sunny climate of the south as well as the quaintness of the old stone houses. They bought homes and then hired the local tradesmen to restore them. In time some of the more picturesque villages became largely owned by outsiders who departed in the fall, leaving the streets deserted during the winter months. These villages were transformed into holiday or show villages without a live-in community. This certainly brought money into areas that were desperately poor, creating work for the trades, but many of the youth still sought their futures elsewhere.

•   •   •

We decided to celebrate Beth's arrival, and hopefully buoy up her spirits, by taking her out for dinner that Saturday. We chose a restaurant named after Barjavel's book, La charrette bleue, located in a village near Nyons. Beth was delighted as we drove over for our seven-o'clock reservation. We arrived to find the restaurant door locked. I looked at my watch.

Marie-Hélène said, "I can see the staff eating at the back table."

"They may not open until seven," I said.

We walked about and returned a few minutes after seven to be warmly welcomed and shown to a table. The waiter came over with a young man at his side and greeted us politely. He handed us menus, then returned to take our orders with the other person still with him.

"Why is that person following him all the time?" Beth asked.

"One's an experienced waiter and the other's his apprentice," Marie-Hélène said. "The apprentice will stay with the waiter the entire evening so that he can learn the correct etiquette. For instance, no one would dare ever bounce over to your table and say, 'Hi, I'm Joe and I'm your server tonight!' as they do in Canada."

"Why not?" Beth asked.

"Well, the position of a waiter or server is viewed as a profession here and is taken very seriously," Marie-Hélène explained. "The etiquette is for discretion at all times. Here's another example: It's considered very bad form to begin clearing the plates at a table until the last person has finished eating."

I added, "There is a rhythm to the event. It is not rushed. The diners set the pace. The order of the courses never varies. Once the principal courses have been served, then cheese or dessert is offered. If the diner wants both, then the cheese will come first. No restaurant will ever suggest coffee or tea until the last dish has been cleared from the table."

Marie-Hélène took a sip of her wine, then said, "We can linger over our coffee or *digestif* and talk without interruption for as long as we want. The waiter will only return when I make eye contact."

Beth laughed and said a little too loudly, "That sounds like flirting." The people at the next table glanced at her.

"The other thing," Marie-Hélène said, "is that the ambiance of the restaurant is quiet and reserved; any music is low so that it is not intrusive. People can carry on conversations without having to raise their voices."

"But isn't it a bit too quiet?" Beth asked in a lower voice.

"The French have a different sense of civility," Marie-Hélène ventured.

"If you are in a hurry, here's a trick," I said. "As small family restaurants only work to a rhythm, if you arrive early you won't get coffee before anyone else in the room. These restaurants have limited staff. They do each course in turn for the entire room. So we found that, if we wanted to eat quickly and leave, the answer was to arrive late and the server will serve us faster to catch up with the rest of the other diners."

The next day Beth strolled into the garden. "I think I'll walk into the village. Is there anything I can get while I'm there?"

"Well, yes, there is something," Marie-Hélène said. "Could you stop at the butcher's and buy a veal roast? I thought that would be nice for dinner tonight. It's Monsieur Poutier, and he's in the main square."

Judging by the bags in Beth's hands when she returned, she'd found most of the boutique shops for tourists as well as the butcher. All the bags landed on the sofa in a heap.

"I'm so upset. On the way back I stopped at the butcher's. It was busy and I stood at what I thought was the tail-end of the line-up. But the butcher ignored me and served other women who came in after me. There was no line-up or queue. They just pushed in front. I couldn't get his attention, so I waved my hand in the air and spoke up over their heads so that he had to hear me and asked, *'Monsieur, avez-vous une queue?'* Everyone stopped talking and began to laugh. I just can't go back there."

Chapter 12

A walk in Nyons

THAT FAMOUS CHARACTER known as the French thief or burglar, the *'voleur'* or *'cambrioleur'*, is alive and well in Provence. We were constantly being advised on how to avoid being robbed. "Never display anything of value." "A purse should be clutched firmly at all times." "Jewellery is a flag attracting the wrong kind of attention." As for the house, one must be sure to lock the doors and windows and close *all* the shutters when going out, even for the shortest periods of time. Clearly, breaking and entering is viewed as a serious problem.

So how does a burglar get into a well-secured house with shutters barred from the inside? That's easy, it seems. A ladder carelessly left in the yard can be used to climb onto the roof. Once there, the cat burglar simply lifts off a few of the roof tiles and *voilà*. Or he brings a small power-operated pry bar, slides it between the shutter and the wall and pops the shutter hinges out of the stone wall. It can be done in seconds.

"I know a couple who went out for several hours and returned home to find the house emptied of all its furniture," Jean told us, shaking his head.

"But how do they know when to strike?" I asked.

"The shutters were all closed, so they knew no one was home."

We listened to the advice and began to act more cautiously. However, closing up the house when we went to the market for a few hours and then reopening everything when we returned home was a lot of work. Too much effort, we thought, and so we slowly became careless. We began to lock the shutters on the ground floor but didn't bother with the shutters on the second floor. Then we stopped closing the shutters on the windows facing the road for our shorter absences. We decided the windows were just too visible and offered a thief no hiding place while breaking in. In fact, we were simply lazy.

Sometime later we noticed that our neighbours were going out and leaving the shutters open on one side of their house. We didn't give this a lot of thought until one day Jean said, "Leaving some shutters open makes the house look occupied. A thief would likely assume there was someone at home and move on to a safer target."

All the same, we heard enough stories to change some of our careless ways. Friends from Canada who owned a house nearby went to Avignon to shop at the mall. Their van was stolen from the parking lot, so they reported the theft to the *gendarmerie* and had the rental agency provide a new van. The next week they returned to Avignon to finish the shopping begun a week earlier, and in disbelief discovered that the new van was stolen in the same mall.

• • •

Buying the *Herald Tribune* had become a daily ritual. It involved walking to the *tabac presse* and saying *"bonjour"* to the lady who took my coins each day. It was normal to run across someone I knew, so formal greetings accompanied by handshakes or *baisers* on the cheeks were inevitably exchanged. Most often I arrived early in the morning at the *tabac presse* and returned home to read the paper with coffee and croissants.

One Wednesday morning I had been working with a tradesman and didn't get to the *tabac presse* until mid-afternoon. So I walked over to La Belle Epoque and found a table on the terrace.

"Un verre de bière pression, s'il vous plaît," I said to the waiter.

Then I leaned back and scanned the headlines before opening the paper. The beer arrived—the first cool sip was always the best. Looking up from reading, I watched the flow of people moving about in their particular daily routines. Nyons is a 'living' village in the sense that the people live, work and shop there. People of all ages—the energetic youth, the frail elderly, the mothers with their babies and the men—all meet on the streets. This was interesting to me, as in Vancouver it is difficult to find a marketplace where people of all ages can be seen going about their daily activities. By and large, the people seen on the streets of Vancouver are adults who drive everywhere. To live in Nyons is to walk.

I recognized a young man sitting by the fountain today, as he did on so many days. His eyes had the wild look of someone not relating to others. Something had agitated him, and a taxi driver who had been sitting in his cab walked over and talked to him. He appeared to calm down and began to wander about the square quite oblivious to much around him, but all the same taking in the activity as best he could. It was as if he did not see or hear the same things other people did. He was disconnected, living in his own world. An elderly person smiled and said hello to him in passing. This caught his attention and provided a moment of recognition before he was distracted by something else. I had seen this before. There was a general understanding that someone nearby should look out for him. More often than not, it was the strangers to the village who created his problems, causing him to lash out in confusion or frustration. A *Nyonsais* would then step over and talk quietly to him, or simply lead him away. He was part of the fabric of the village life, just as everyone else.

• • •

After the heat of the day, we decided to walk into the village to show Beth around and further distract her from her problems.

"We can look for a restaurant with a terrace," I said, "and it's so warm I'm just wearing a T-shirt, shorts and sandals." Marie-Hélène and Beth liked the idea and dressed the same way.

I closed the gate and the three of us ambled down the hill. The evening air was still, the sun had lost its heat and cast a yellow glow on the landscape.

We passed Yvette and Gilles' farm with its vineyards and apricot orchards. Yvette was in the garden.

"I've got to have a quick word with her about Myrtille," Marie-Hélène said as she dashed up their driveway. While they chatted, Beth and I walked over to a narrow bridge and waited.

I looked down at the trickle of water in the almost dry riverbed. "A thunderstorm in July turned this into a raging torrent of water nearly overflowing its banks for a few hours, and then it settled back to this small stream the next day."

Marie-Hélène had finished her chat and caught up to us. "I had to tell her how Myrtille and the kittens are doing."

We continued across the bridge, so narrow that only one car crossed at a time, and then started along a road with a long sweeping curve. "This was at one time part of the railway line to Nyons. It was built around the turn of the century and was removed in the 1950s. Just ahead you can see the old station. Apparently there was a roundhouse as well to turn the train around to go back in the other direction. The station is now a government office."

"This must have been an isolated place," Beth said. "How did they get anywhere?"

"You've nailed it. Before the railway, travel was on foot or on horseback, or by carriage for those who could afford it. They used the roads or trails running between the farms. The railway opened up the region. The outside world reached here faster and easier, and the villagers and farmers were able to get out to other areas. Before that, most people rarely travelled farther than the next village."

"Wow. I had never really thought about it. I got here from Canada by plane, train and your car all in one day," Beth said.

"It took just a hundred years to accomplish the change. The gas-guzzling automobiles arrived in the forties and fifties, displacing the need for the train system."

We strolled three-abreast along the road until we reached an intersection of five roads. In the middle is a circle the drivers have to drive around.

"That's called a 'rond-point.' It allows numerous roads to intersect without any vehicles having to stop. The rule is a driver simply yields to the car on his left and then exits the rond-point on the road he wants."

I pointed and said, "Oh, look over there, that puff of smoke. It's from the lavender press, where oil is extracted from the flowers and distilled into lavender essence. Can you smell it? It permeates the village in the summer."

Beth sniffed the air. "Yes, I can. It's wonderful."

"Those mountains to the north protect the village from the mistral wind. In turn they hold the heat of the sun, giving Nyons a warm microclimate."

We walked on into the main village square with its towering shade trees. On the one side was La Belle Epoque where we lunched regularly. On the other was the cinema with a billboard advertising a Gérard Depardieu movie currently playing.

"That four-storey wall ahead of us with the huge portal was built by the Romans. I was told that the wall was so thick that after the Romans left the villagers dug out the rubble inside and built these apartments in the space. They cut holes for doors and windows. Even the round towers at either end are apartments now."

I motioned, "Come over to this portal and look up here. These big holes are where the iron hinges for the massive wooden gates were mounted into the wall. Just the holes remain today."

Both Beth and Marie-Hélène were listening, so I continued. "At one time Nyons was a trading centre, as it sits on the edge of the Pre-Alps and the Rhône Valley. People travelled down from the hills on foot or by donkeys and carts to trade in the weekly market.

"Technically speaking, Nyons is now too large to be a village. It long ago outgrew the old village contained behind the Roman walls. But it doesn't function like a city either, as the economy is still largely agrarian. The population is about 8,000 and swells to over twice that in the summer with visitors."

We turned to our left and began to walk up steep stone stairs between the stone and shuttered houses, along winding narrow lanes. After a few turns I pointed out a massive iron gate, behind which rose a structure of over three storeys. "That is Château Féodal. Have you ever heard of Madame de Sévigné, who lived at Château Grignan and wrote her famous letters to her daughter?"

Beth shook her head.

"Here at Château Féodal the châtelaine, Lydie Marshall, teaches cooking and writes her cookbooks. She's a charming lady who was born in France, raised in the Midwest of the United States, and then lived in New York for years before returning to France with her husband to settle in Nyons. They restored the château. It even has a shaded swimming pool set in a lush, multi-tiered garden that would rival the Hanging Gardens of Babylon.

"Some people say that Hannibal led his army through Nyons on his way to sack Rome, but there is no direct evidence to back this up. Clearly the Moors reached this far into France, as they built the watchtower that overlooks the village."

I was tiring of the tour-guide role, so we walked in silence down a few more lanes, coming out beside a stone bridge rising high above the river. With one last effort I explained, "This is a Roman-style bridge built in the fourteenth century. It is a single span of over forty metres, one of the longest in Europe."

We walked across, the three of us taking up the entire width of the bridge. "Over there, Marie-Hélène took a photo of the riders in the Tour de France with Lance Armstrong wearing the yellow jersey."

As we started back, a small car approached from the other side, so we pressed ourselves against the stone guardrail on the bridge to let it pass.

"There's a street of restaurants ahead. Let's take a look at their menus. What're you in the mood for, Beth?"

"I don't know. What is there?" she replied vaguely.

We entered a street where a dozen or more restaurants spread out their tables and chairs onto the road, until only a narrow path down the centre was left for cars to pass.

"Well, there are French, Thai, Chinese and Italian," I pointed out. One establishment offering hamburgers had a moustached cowboy in leather chaps with a gun in his belt crudely painted on the façade.

We walked past each one, reading the menus at the front doors. Many people were seated and eating or drinking, while others milled about on the remaining space down the middle of the road, trying to make up their minds as well.

"Do you see anything?" Marie-Hélène asked Beth.

"Uh, not really," was the only reply.

Then we passed an African restaurant with loud drums playing and a very dark-skinned man serving tables. Beth stopped and looked inside at the drummer in a corner playing with his head nodding from side to side.

"This looks kind of interesting," she said.

"Do you want to try it?" Marie-Hélène offered.

Beth was already studying the menu, one leg moving to the beat of the drums. "I don't recognize anything, but I've never had African food."

"Let's try it," Marie-Hélène said decidedly and motioned to the waiter.

The outdoor seating was taken, so we were shown to a table next to an African shield and several spears resting in a corner. Afghan carpets covered the floor. African images were painted on the walls and ebony carvings occupied a shelf. The throb of the drums reverberated like a physical force in the small room. A heavy aroma of spiced food emanated from the kitchen.

Beth looked around. "This place has real atmosphere."

The menu favoured couscous with a choice of meats or vegetables. We ordered our dishes and red wine. The wine arrived in a clay jug along with three small glass tumblers. We sat, taking in the rhythm of the music, not trying to talk over it.

The food arrived on large oval metal trays. Each contained couscous, chickpeas, fava beans and a variety of other vegetables. The waiter placed a small bowl of hot sauce in the middle of the table. Just as we began to eat the drummer took a break and the buzz of conversation rose to take its place.

We had ordered lamb, rabbit and chicken dishes.

"Let's share," Marie-Hélène declared.

"Okay," agreed Beth, and we began swapping portions.

Beth tasted the hot sauce and quickly had a sip of wine.

The drummer was back, and after stuffing a packet of cigarettes into his shirt pocket began playing again. During her slow moments in the kitchen a dark-skinned woman emerged wearing an apron, briefly undulated provocatively to the beat of the drums, and then returned to her cooking.

The dessert was a Moroccan cinnamon–flavoured custard.

We left the restaurant after dark and walked home in the cool air. The cicadas, waiting for the heat of the next day, had long since gone silent. Even the cock at Yvette and Gilles' farm had turned in for the night.

Chapter 13
The cicadas' song, and a truce breaks out

After two weeks with Beth we had come to accept that every conversation would wind its way back to her current state of affairs. She was one of those people who always appeared to have a handkerchief in her hand, whether or not there was one actually there. For a short while a tea towel served the purpose, but she successfully managed to have other things in her hands, even when the tea towel could have been useful. Generally it was a glass of wine. These weren't conversations where I was expected to be a lot of use, so I tended to be on the periphery, caught between listening in and impolitely ignoring it all. After putting away the dishes, I could leave the room and not be missed.

As we settled into bed a few days later, Marie-Hélène turned to me and said, "Beth asked if she could use our computer to e-mail her husband and discuss settlement of the assets. I said yes."

Days passed with e-mails going back and forth but without

any sign of progress, judging by the damp mood Beth exuded. A certain amount of huffing and pouting or simply despair coloured the air. Marie-Hélène and I kept ourselves busy and out of the way as much as possible.

"Yikes!"

Marie-Hélène heard this exclamation while stripping wallpaper on the ground floor. She put down her scraper and ran up the stairs. Beth was standing with a cup of coffee in her hand and looking down at the sofa.

"I'm so sorry! I've spilled coffee on the sofa."

She went to the kitchen counter and came back with a dry tea towel and began to rub the stained fabric. Marie-Hélène looked at this and got a wet cloth with liquid soap and began to rub out the stain. After some minutes of effort the stain seemed to have lifted. A large wet patch remained in the centre of one cushion.

"I hope it's okay."

"I'm sure it will be—when I bought the couch last month I was told it was stain-proofed," Marie-Hélène offered.

"I guess I should read on the balcony, shouldn't I?"

Marie-Hélène smiled and reassured her it would be alright, then retreated to the ground floor again, ruminating on her new couch. Marie-Hélène, in her infinite kindness, accepted that Beth was going through a difficult time.

The cicadas' shrill song, rising and falling in almost deafening waves, filled the hot summer days. Then suddenly it was interrupted by the crowing of the cock down the hill.

We had begun to regulate our days by the sun. As the temperature rose into the high thirties, normal activities had to be abandoned.

The shutters on the house were closed before the sun became

unbearable in order to keep the cool night air indoors, and then opened all night to create air movement in order to sleep. Sometimes near dawn the sweet scent of jasmine would drift through the bedroom windows. Our days slowed to a crawl; drives in the air-conditioned car became pleasant, but the villages turned into ovens as the sun heated the stone walls and the paved streets. The heat made us drowsy by midday. After lunch we soon found ourselves settling in for afternoon naps. The shuttered bedroom was cool and still. The days of rambling walks exploring nearby villages came to a stop.

We began lunching at restaurants with swimming pools; a quick dip and then lunch on the terrace. I had built an outdoor shower in a corner of the garden, half hidden by the trees where the olive wood had once been stacked. The plumber ran a water line from the house. I put up a small, six-sided canvas tent top that I supported on wood poles and then enclosed with a bamboo screen, creating a secluded garden spot to retreat to in order to cool off. The shower head, a foot in diameter, rained water from overhead. At midday the water ran from hot to cold, as the pipe was partly exposed to the sun. Taking an outdoor shower became a refreshingly cool respite from the August sun.

In Provence, cicadas are sold in all sizes and colours of porcelain, metal, clay and plastic. Yet I had never seen a live one, despite the racket they make. This didn't turn out to be the easiest thing to do. The moment I approached a cicada it fell silent. I searched the nearby trees and shrubs but gave up. When I moved away, in a minute or two its song would begin again. After several unsuccessful attempts, I changed my technique. When I approached and it stopped singing, I stood still and waited. Soon it began again. I moved a bit closer, and when the sound stopped I stopped as well. Finally I knew I must be within reach of it. I slowly scanned up and down the tree trunk next to me and still couldn't see it. Possibly it was on the other side. Then I noticed a slight bulge that blended perfectly with the rough grey bark of the tree. I made out the form. It was about two inches in length with long, transparent wings like a grasshopper. It didn't move. The camouflage was so good that only its own movement was likely to give it away. In silence we watched each other. Then I moved off, and soon afterwards it once more struck up its raucous chord.

A look of frustration was all over Beth's face. "E-mails just don't do it—can I use your phone? I've got to get through to him," she said, displaying some anxiety. And so, with the nine-hour time difference between Nyons and Vancouver, just as we had finished our work for the day and begun to relax the phone was carried off to a more private corner of the house.

"I'll pay you for the long-distance calls once the bill comes in," was offered. Unfortunately France Telecom doesn't offer discounts for long-distance calls like the North American telephone companies, and we knew the bill was rising by the day.

Whenever possible I would take early morning or evening drives searching for stones. The wall rose slowly, from a single course to three, and I was learning the skills for stacking stones at a seven-per-cent slope off vertical. But I was running out of places to look for suitable stones. On a drive up Mont Ventoux I noticed that rock outcroppings that had come loose in the winter offered good but small rewards—but that was getting far afield. I wondered if that may have been why the dry stone walls I studied had the smaller stones at the top.

The work in the new guest suite had progressed in fits and starts, with the tile floor having been laid by the mason and the plasterboard installed by another artisan. That in itself had been a challenge; we had e-mailed back and forth and finally fixed a date for the plasterboard work. When the date arrived and Marie-Hélène called him, he said he was busy. Marie-Hélène reminded him that the e-mails set a date we all had agreed on. He replied that she had him in a box. Marie-Hélène laughed and replied that she liked him in a box. He was amused by that, and so that weekend found time to do the work.

"Have you called the electrician?" Marie-Hélène asked me.

"Yes, two days ago and again today. All I get is a recorded message at his office. No one returns my calls."

We left it at that and waited.

François and I spent long hours in the garden together moving plants, pruning them and maintaining the watering system. We gardened and he instructed me in French. When I said that pruning the tree was my *derrière* job for the day, he laughed and slapped his rear end.

"The word is *dernier, Jeem.*"

"*Il est chaud aujourd'hui,*" I said, wiping my brow.

"*Ce n'est pas correct, Jeem,*" he responded. "*L'expression est 'Il fait chaud' ou 'J'ai chaud.'*"

François was one of those rare people who seemed unaffected by the heat. He just kept on gardening in his usual manner in the direct sun. While we talked, Beth stepped from the outdoor shower enclosure and began to walk barefoot across the coarse gravel patio with just a towel wrapped around her middle. As she walked gingerly along, she stepped on something, let out a yelp and jumped, letting slip the towel. She snatched it up quickly, rewrapping herself, and made the best of a dash on her toes for the open door. François paused from his work, suppressing his laughter, his eyes following her until she disappeared indoors.

"Merde . . ." He got up off his knees, walked over to the shower, pulled the chain and held his head under the stream of water. It was a hot day.

We had heard stories about the fabled French bureaucracy but had not encountered it until a letter arrived in the mail one day. A government department wanted us to state how many television sets we owned. This seemed like an odd question, so Marie-Hélène asked Suzette about it, who replied that television sets were taxed annually and we had to reply. Fortunately we didn't own one, so we replied accordingly. Several weeks went by and another letter arrived in our mailbox. This time the government agency asked us to please certify that we did not own a television. Clearly our first letter had met with some scepticism. We again replied in the negative, certified the form and mailed it. For the next few months we half-expected that at any time the 'television inspector' would appear at our door with a warrant to search the house. I was never quite sure whether I was relieved or disappointed that no one came.

We had been away most of that Sunday at a festival in the village of Cairanne, but on returning it was clear something had happened. There were cars parked on the road next to the driveway up to Faustin Buisson's house. One was a medical van, another belonged to the *gendarmerie*. A few men stood talking. It took some time for the vehicles to leave.

Suzette, in her courteous way, called to tell Marie-Hélène that Monsieur Buisson had died in his home. Apparently it was heart failure. What had drawn attention that something was wrong was the whining and barking of his dog.

The next day the son arrived on his motorcycle. He stayed and made arrangements for the funeral. Several days later, Jean, wearing a black suit, and Suzette, with a hat on, made their way to the village to pay their final respects.

The phone was ringing, waking me.

"It's probably for *me*" I heard Beth holler.

Marie-Hélène rolled over. "What time is it?"

I glanced at the clock. "Two in the morning!"

We could hear Beth's muffled conversation at the other end of the house.

Over breakfast, Beth explained, "He forgot about the time difference. I told him, and he said I should let you know how sorry he is."

We ran into Madame Joule, the realtor, in the Thursday *marché*. She gave the strong impression of a woman with little time to waste.

I said, "Pierre Luc says he is selling his property."

"*Bof!* I can't get him to come in to sign the *notaire's* papers. Twice now he hasn't kept appointments. I even got him more than the property is worth."

"But isn't he contractually obligated to sell?"

"Sure he is—but try getting him to do so. He can be sued for breach of contract. I hold a deposit, so the deal is *sûr*."

Faustin's son began to return more frequently. We learned from Suzette that his name was Marius. He worked in one of the large electronics retailing stores in Aix. She said he was clever, and not of the same temperament as Pierre Luc at all, even though they had grown up as the best of friends. Within a month Marius was spending more than just weekends at the house. His companion was often with him. He seemed to have a considerable amount of business to do in the village.

Another vehicle began to appear about this time. I was standing on the balcony clearing dishes after lunch when a decrepit bright-green Citroën 2CV raced up the road with a small girl standing on the passenger side, her face pressed to the windshield. The car vanished around the next bend in the road. I wondered if this could be Pierre Luc's daughter, but I had been told she was in Paris. As the days passed, I noticed the car with the girl speed by more often.

Beth rushed onto the balcony where we were sipping wine that evening. "He's coming to see me!"

"Your husband?"

"Yes, yes," she said. "He's coming here."

We stared blankly. Clearly she was digesting it too.

"He wants me to meet him in Paris, so I'm going to take the train on Tuesday."

That was two days away and gave us time to adjust to the idea of having our house back, along with the computer and the telephone.

"Can you drive me to Avignon?"

"Of course we can, Beth. That's wonderful news!"

The train station in Avignon is one of the masterpieces of modern art the French are building along the high-speed TGV routes. However, there was no parking within 75 metres of the station, so all luggage had to be carried or dragged across the hot sunny gauntlet and up a sloping ramp to the *voie*, where the train could be boarded. The three of us stood there waiting. As the TGV came into sight, we positioned ourselves at the spot where the right coach would stop and the door open. Every stop was measured in a precise number of seconds, then the doors unceremoniously closed and the train was immediately in motion again. A miscalculation, like standing at the wrong spot on the platform, could result in not boarding at all and being left watching the train pull away from the platform. We weren't going to let that happen.

I positioned the suitcases to block others until we had both cases on board, but first those getting off had to be let by. Then the rush to board began. I pushed Beth up the first step and shoved a case at her. She could barely move it, so a man behind her lifted it the rest of the way onboard. I immediately shoved the other case at her and she tugged it up the next step. We had done our hugging and goodbyes on the platform and so we waved enthusiastically, blew kisses, and then lost sight of each other as the crush of other passengers forced her back from the door.

As all the windows are heavily tinted, we couldn't see inside. We stood there waving at our reflections in the glass until the train pulled away and gathered speed.

Chapter 14
Another truce

AUGUST CAN BE the hottest month of the year, with temperatures hovering between 35 and 40 °C each day. The cicadas seemed to be the only things enjoying the heat. Most Frenchmen wisely consider it too hot to work and take their annual *vacances*. Even the swimming-pool salesmen go south to the coast—it's too late in the season to install one for this summer. By September customers will be clamouring to plan a pool for next year.

In the summer heat, the population of the cities drains away and business slows or stops entirely. The place to be is the seacoast. So the exodus from the cities turns into a slow-moving crush of bumper-to-bumper cars, vans, caravans, powerful motorcycles and transport trucks, all gridlocked on hot pavement amid their exhaust fumes. The A7 Autoroute du Soleil, which is normally the high-speed corridor down the Rhône Valley, becomes a traffic jam of angry drivers and cranky passengers who aren't getting where they want to be fast enough.

The daily news reports the inevitable accidents that bring all four lanes of traffic to a stop for hours while police, ambulances and tow trucks try to wind their way through the jam, pick up the pieces and clear the road. Even the most stoic travellers arrive at their destinations to start their vacations in the foulest of moods.

On the Mediterranean all accommodation, from the luxury hotels to the B & Bs, is occupied. There is jostling room only on the beaches. One returning villager complained that there was so much suntan lotion used it fouled the beaches. It conjured the image of hot dogs roasting on an open grill.

For us, the pattern of life changed as the temperature rose. Tennis, if played at all, took place in the early morning before the court surface became so hot that we felt our runners would melt underfoot. The routine of closing all the shutters at dawn and reopening them at dusk remained in effect. Exposure to the direct sun felt like a hammer blow. We moved from one pocket of shade to the next. The outdoor markets emptied earlier than usual. Some villagers retreated to the mountains.

Driving was comfortable so long as the car was air-conditioned, but the interior of a car left in the sun heated to oven temperatures within minutes. Any hope of finding parking in the shade was futile.

Tabitha and Myrtille had made peace since the arrival of the kittens. During the day they alternated between basking indolently in the sun and seeking out shady nooks. Myrtille's kittens had grown old enough for her to escape their constant demands. They remained in our bedroom, sleeping or playing. While Myrtille stayed closer to her litter, Tabitha wandered in the shade of the garden, sniffing the profusion of pink valerian blossoms, darting after bees and other insects, or stalking a bird.

This was not a month to expect to have a call returned about unfinished work. However, François arrived faithfully each Friday, and Albin put in a few appearances.

One Wednesday I answered the ringing telephone.

"Hello, Gordon. This is Dave—Dave Mallard. How are you?"

"We're well, Dave—"

"We're here in Marseilles," he continued before I could say more. "We just got off the cruise ship and we've got a few days. I thought we should call and say hello."

"It's good to hear from you—"

"We've rented a car and will be driving about," he once again interceded.

"We'd really like to drop by and say hello to you and your wife, and see what your place looks like."

"By all means, Dave. When do you have in mind?"

"Well, if it's alright with you, we could be up there by two or three this afternoon. From what I can see on the map you're about two hours north of here."

We hung up and I went to find Marie-Hélène.

"Dave and Dot Mallard are coming by this afternoon. They're in Marseilles," I told her.

"The Mallards?"

"Yes, he's been an important client of mine."

I let the thought work its way through her head.

"Okay, I had better plan dinner." She put down her paint brush and peeled off the rubber gloves.

"Can you run down to Intermarché and buy some rabbit, potatoes, vegetables of some sort, and something for dessert? We'll eat in the garden."

By four o'clock no one had arrived. Then a station wagon came up the road with Dave's wife looking out the window holding a map in her hand. I waved and her face brightened into a smile. Then I saw two children in the back seat and the luggage behind them.

"Sorry to be so late," Dave explained. "We got lost coming through Carpentras. The signs in that place are atrocious. We must have gone around it three times before we found the right road out. . . ."

We all shook hands and kissed each other.

"These two are Agatha and Behan. She's seven and he's five." The children were already sizing up the garden for things to do.

"You must be tired from all that driving. Can I get you something to drink?" I offered.

"Yeah, a beer would be great. How about you, Dot?"

Dot settled on a glass of white wine and I poured glasses of Orangina for the children.

"You've got a pretty nice place here," Dave said. "Looks spacious."

Marie-Hélène overheard that and turned to Dot. "Would you like to see it?"

The first room we entered from the patio had a painter's drop sheet spread on the floor, along with paint cans, a roller and brushes. Three of the walls had been scraped clean of wallpaper, revealing grey concrete, and the fourth wall had a primer coat of paint on it. After a tour of the upstairs we moved downstairs again to the new guest suite. The room was empty. There wasn't even a chair to sit on. Bare wires dangled from the walls and ceiling.

Just then a loud grinding noise erupted. Albin and his assistant were drilling a hole in the outside wall to attach the iron pergola to the house. Dust clouds rolled in the air. We waved at him and he waved back still holding the drill against the wall. They were covered in dust. It stuck to their clothing and caked on their faces in the heat of the day.

"They'll quit for the day fairly soon. Let's go around to the other patio where it's a bit quieter," I suggested, moving everyone in the other direction.

The children had disappeared into the garden in search of something to do. Behan had found Myrtille and was pursuing her through the rosemary. Just then Agatha appeared with her hair and dress all wet. As she walked her shoes squished.

Dot rushed over to her. "Agie, what happened to you, you poor thing?"

"I pulled a chain over there in that tent and it rained on me," she whined.

Marie-Hélène brought out a towel and Dot rubbed Agatha down. "The dress will dry in no time in this heat," Marie-Hélène volunteered.

The four of us sat around the garden table and sipped our drinks.

"We were hoping you could stay for dinner," Marie-Hélène offered.

"Oh, that would be wonderful," Dot cooed.

Now came the important question.

"Do you have a place to stay tonight?" I asked.

"No, we don't," Dave said, looking a bit sheepish.

"Nyons has a nice hotel. Maybe we should call over and see about a room," I offered.

Dave concurred, so the two of us went inside to use the telephone.

As I came outside again, Behan was standing next to Dot. She was examining scratches on both his cheeks.

"What happened?" I asked.

Marie-Hélène said, "Behan caught Myrtille."

He was whimpering, but no real blood had been drawn.

Dave ignored all this and wanted to know what it was really like to live in Provence. Dot and Marie-Hélène went off to the kitchen to prepare dinner.

The evening air was cooler and we pushed two tables together on the patio. Dinner was brought out on trays and set on a side table. We were to serve ourselves. Dot sent the children over to the table to start.

"What is this, Mom?" Agatha asked, looking at the rabbit.

"It's chicken, my dear," Dot told her.

Behan busily loaded up his plate and then headed for the table to eat.

Agatha stood looking at the dishes. "Is that butter or margarine on the potatoes?"

"It's olive oil, dear. We're in Provence and that's what they use here."

Agatha took small helpings of everything and went to sit next to Behan.

When the last of us sat down, Marie-Hélène said, "I'd like to make a toast to good friends getting together for dinner. Welcome to *Les Oliviers*." The glasses clinked and everyone started in to eat. Agatha was picking at her food, tasting but not eating. Behan had no problem and was already climbing off his chair to get more food.

"Agie's a bit tired from all the travel today. She'll feel better with a little rest," Dot said.

"Wow, this *lapin* is delicious, Marie-Hélène! I've never had it before," Dave said enthusiastically.

Dot looked at him with a hard stare.

"What's the matter? Did I say something wrong?" he demanded.

Dot motioned with her hand to leave it alone, but it was too late.

"Mom, what's *lapin?*" Agatha asked

"It's a French name for what we're having tonight dear—is your dress dry yet, sweetie?" Dot replied.

Agatha had her teeth into something now and wasn't going to let go.

"But what is it? What's the English name?"

Dave said, "It's rabbit."

Agatha's face contorted into a mask of horror.

"Are we eating a bunny?" Her voice had gone squeaky.

"My *gawd*, Dave, did you *have* to say that?" Dot snapped.

Dave withdrew a bit, realizing his mistake. But by now Agatha was actually changing colour and squirming in her chair. Her eyes began to water and then turn red. She rose and dashed into the house with Dot in pursuit. Marie-Hélène followed.

In a few minutes, Marie-Hélène returned.

"I made Agatha a peanut-butter sandwich and poured her a glass of milk."

Sometime after that Dot came out and sat down. Dave remained quieter for a while.

After dinner, I saw them down to the hotel and returned to find Marie-Hélène doing dishes.

"I drove them past the new swimming-pool complex in Nyons and suggested the children would enjoy it there tomorrow."

Tabitha returned home sometime before dawn. Myrtille had moved under the bed with her kittens.

On Friday morning the Mallards drove up the hill and parked in our driveway.

"We just wanted to drop by and say we are on our way and

how much we enjoyed dinner the other night," Dave said.

"Thank you," I replied.

I looked at the children in the back seat. They were a bright pink colour and Behan's nose had already begun to peel, revealing red beneath. They looked somewhat haggard, no doubt feeling the first effects of sunburn and possibly sunstroke as well.

"That's some funny attitude they have over there at the pool," Dave said.

I looked at him quizzically. "What do you mean?"

"When we tried to get in, the man at the gate said we weren't dressed properly. I was wearing a pair of boxer swimming trunks and Dot had on a bra top and shorts. He said we weren't dressed in a sanitary manner. After a lot of effort he let Dot roll up her shorts, but I had to go and buy a Speedo," he exclaimed.

Dot laughed at this.

Dave went on, "In Canada, Dot won't let me wear a Speedo— something about my stomach not suiting it."

Dot had to say something too. "The kids loved the slides and ran around in the sun all day. Dave spent his time ogling a full-bodied woman suntanning topless."

A look passed between them.

Dave put the conversation back on course, "Well, we only stopped by to say thanks for the dinner the other night. We're off to see the Pont du Gard near Nîmes and then will catch our flight home tomorrow."

We wished them well and waved as they drove off.

•   •   •

By late August the sale of Pierre Luc's property had not been concluded. The farm had remained unattended all summer. Whenever I saw him coming and going, his shoulders were slumped and he walked slowly, as if he were busy following the flow of his own thoughts. He was a sad sight.

Then one day I looked up the hill to see Pierre Luc's wife on a ladder in the corner of the orchard, pruning the trees. The girl I had seen in the green 2CV was chasing Pierre Luc's dog. He was there too, helping to pick up the cuttings. Later in the day he walked down the road and I hollered, *"Bonjour."*

He looked up and came over to shake hands. Before I could say anything, he said, "My wife, Fanny, is back from Paris. She says it's so hot on the streets that no one goes out. She couldn't afford to live in central Paris and the *banlieues* around Paris are depressing, with all kinds of ethnic unrest. Nobody knew each other, even the neighbours. She couldn't let Violette out of her sight and Violette got all pouty and cranky. Fanny couldn't stand it. The only available work was depressing factory jobs or menial clerical help."

"Is she back to stay?"

"Beh voui—je pense," he said. He looked a bit brighter and even his dog wagged its tail more vigorously.

I shouldn't have asked the next question, but my curiosity won out. "Does she know you have a deal to sell the farm?"

"Non," he said, lowering his head. "She's back, and I couldn't tell her."

I was struck speechless for a moment. "It's good she's back," was all I could come up with. I didn't want to contemplate the looming disaster of the property sale.

To furnish the guest suite, we returned in late August to a favourite weekend past-time—haunting the *vide-greniers* and village antique *marchés* and stopping by the *brocantes*.

In Sablet we came across a stall selling a bow-fronted end table made from fruitwood. After the usual haggling over the price, it was loaded in the back of the car. All it needed was a coat of wax and polishing.

We found the second end table at a *vide-grenier* in a small village. The young couple selling it couldn't have liked its old look. They wanted *le moderne*.

Finding a small desk was not so easy. We came upon several that weren't satisfactory. One was badly overpriced, the other beyond restoring. Buying antiques requires a lot of patience and a dash of luck. The desk we settled on was the right size and price, but it lacked the charm we had hoped for. A week later we saw a much better one, but by then it was too late. Then we found an old chair that matched the desk and set it off perfectly. Our eye for *provençal* furniture was improving.

Chapter 15
The harvest

IT WAS MID-MORNING on the last Friday in August and François hadn't arrived yet. He normally came at exactly seven. Then I heard the sound of a truck labouring hard coming up the road. It was losing speed on the hill, but then the transmission was shifted into a lower gear. However, the engine was still under considerable strain. Stepping out onto the balcony, I looked down to see François's truck inching along. The truck bed was loaded with stones. It reached our driveway, stopped, then reversed and slowly backed up to our gate. François hopped out.

"Bonjour, François."

He looked up and smiled at me.

I ran down the stairs and met him at the gate he was already opening. We exchanged the usual formal greeting, and then he put his hand on the side of the truck.

"Regardez," he said, and then watched me with a twinkle in his eyes.

I looked over the metal side into the truck box and saw a mound of stones at least three feet high. I began to wonder what this was going to cost me. Stones in Provence, although plentiful, were expensive when ordered from a quarry, not to mention the cost for loading and delivery.

François seemed to read my mind, for with a look of glee and pride he said, *"C'est libre."*

"Ce n'est pas possible," I replied, yet hoping it was true.

"Mais oui—rien," He patted the side of his truck. "This is for you. You need stones for the wall." I looked again at the load while he began to explain.

"I was at the quarry for the district this morning and the quarrier was complaining that the dynamiter had blown the rock into pieces too small for the boulders needed to shore up the riverbanks. He was about to dump the rocks down the hillside. I asked for a load and he was delighted to get rid of it. Two scoops with the loader filled my truck."

I looked again at the load of broken rock that was perfect for a dry stone wall.

"François, vous êtes extraordinaire!"

He backed the truck into the driveway and lowered one side-panel. All we had to do was lift the stones into a wheelbarrow, roll each load around to the other side of the house, and dump it on the gravel patio. I could then select the stones one by one as I built the wall.

It took the two of us most of the day to move it all. By evening I appreciated François' strong physical condition. I was exhausted and simply glad to have the job done—or so I thought.

The next morning I tried to get out of bed. When my feet reached the floor a sharp pain in my back stopped any further movement. I tried to push myself upright with my hands but found that some muscles in my arms didn't respond. I sank back on the bed, my back in a spasm. My arms were sore and my hands didn't want to form a fist. The day turned into agony as the stiffness spread to other muscles. My back remained bent. It felt as if my body had aged twenty years overnight.

The pile of stones remained untouched on the patio.

* * *

The days of September were getting shorter, marking the decline of summer. The vast blue fields of lavender around Nyons had been cut and the blossoms sent to the press to be distilled into lavender essence. It was the season for harvesting apples, pears, quince, and the last of the figs. There was an abundance of varieties, all ripening at slightly different times and offering a range of flavours. Children gathered beneath the chestnut trees to stuff their pockets with the fallen nuts.

The evenings darkened earlier, and instead of sitting in the garden after dinner we gradually moved our activities indoors.

In the vineyards of Provence the grape clusters had turned purple on the vines and the *vignerons* anxiously watched the sky, hoping no rain would fall before the *ban des vendanges* was announced and they could begin the harvest. If they ignored the ban and started early their coveted AOC status could be lost, and the wine would have to be sold as common *vin de pays*, which meant less profit. If they waited and rain intervened, the grapes would swell with water and lose concentration. As the success of the harvest turned on the date the *ban* was lifted, the announcement brought everyone to the villages for festivities. We heard about the event in Vinsobres and drove over the hilltop, arriving to find the streets crowded with people. Some, dressed in period costumes, were putting on skits and dances. The traditional broad-brimmed black hats worn by the men in the vineyards were visible everywhere.

Vinsobres, perched on its own hill, is a village with cobblestone streets so narrow and steep that cars are prohibited. The crowd milled around in a mood of celebration and then began to gather in the square in front of the mayor's office. Cheering started as a man pushed his way to the stage wearing nothing but grape vines wrapped around his waist and over his shoulders. A wreath of grape leaves crowned his head, and on his back hung a small wooden keg. Bacchus had arrived.

The crowd pushed toward him, holding out their wineglasses. He reached down to his waist and into the leaves, pulled out a plastic hose, and wine poured out, filling all the glasses within reach.

Amid the dancing on the stage and the acting out of harvest skits a bugle blew behind us. Everyone turned to see a procession of men in red and gold ankle-length gowns carrying long staffs coming out of the mayor's office. The wine confrérie was here to bless the vintage. After enduring a long speech, everyone turned to the tables laden with wines from the *vignerons* of Vinsobres. The opportunity had never been so good to compare Vinsobres wines, but after tasting a few we just joined in the party, celebrating the harvest like everyone around us.

The ban having been lifted meant that it was time for me to help Monsieur Ladoux up the road harvest his grapes. Early one morning I saw him arrive at his vineyard on a tractor with a large metal hopper in tow. I put on some work clothes and a baseball cap and walked over. There was another man with him. Monsieur Ladoux gave me a wide smile and introduced us. Then he looked at my cap and walked over to the tractor and came back with one of the traditional broad-brimmed black hats the French once wore for the harvest. He pointed at my cap and said, "*Trop petit. C'est mieux comme ça.*"

I noticed that the other man was wearing the same kind of black hat but Monsieur Ladoux stayed with his cap. I tried on the hat and he handed me a pair of gloves and a *sécateur* that looked like snub-nosed scissors.

"*C'est la première fois?*" he asked in his thick patois.

I nodded yes.

"*Okay, regardez-moi,*" he said, and walked over to a vine that was espaliered along a wire some thirty inches off the ground.

He half-bent at the knees, reached through the leaves and held a grape cluster in his left hand. With his right hand he found the stem of the cluster and put the *sécateur* blades on it. "*Coupez.*"

The cluster fell into his hand.

"Don't bend at the waist. You won't last an hour if you do. Besides, the grapes will fall out of the basket. Use your knees."

He picked up a wicker basket tapered in a cone shape with straps and showed me how to put it on my back. *"Pour les raisins,"* he said, and made a motion of dropping something over his shoulder.

Now that all the instructions were completed, he pointed to a row of vines. *"Commencez-là."*

The other man was already working his way up another row and dropping grape clusters into his basket. I walked over and started to work. The first few clusters were easy enough and I felt pretty good about the project. Then Monsieur Ladoux came over and said, *"Regardez."* He lifted up some leaves on one of the vines I had already worked on and showed me a cluster of grapes I hadn't seen.

"Oh, pardon," I said sheepishly. I walked back and snipped the cluster, dropping it over my shoulder.

As the morning progressed my knees slowly began to ache and my quadriceps seemed to harden and become less flexible. I tried bending my back but remembered the advice not to do just that. After several hours I had harvested about half the row while I noticed that the other worker had already moved onto his second row. Monsieur Ladoux had done so as well. My back did not straighten as easily with the weight of the grapes in the basket. I had emptied it a number of times into the hopper. I had to stop more frequently to straighten up and stretch. The other two just stayed low to the vines and kept on working. I tried to pick up the pace so that it wouldn't look as if I was falling behind. I had to lift the hat to wipe the perspiration from my brow before it ran down my face to sting my eyes.

"Déjeuner!" Monsieur Ladoux called briskly at noon, and marched over to the tractor. He almost sounded animated by the idea.

I straightened slowly to an erect stance and headed to our house, where Marie-Hélène had lunch ready.

"Well, how's it going?" she asked.

I sat down, realizing it was the first time I had done so since early morning.

"Well enough," I offered. "We should finish the vineyard this afternoon." I wasn't going to admit the way I felt.

"Oh, let me get a towel."

"Why?" I asked.

"You've got grape juice all over your back."

The afternoon progressed and so did the aches. My back felt like I had an oak timber in it, and my legs needed constant changing of position as I searched new ways to reach down to the vines. Even though I seemed to be finding a rhythm to the work, I wasn't catching up to the pace of Monsieur Ladoux and the other worker. I was even beginning to feel grateful that the hailstorm had wiped out part of the vineyard.

By four in the afternoon we had finished. Monsieur Ladoux looked pleased, shook my hand, and patted me on my tender back, which was unusual friendliness for the normally reserved French. I put the *sécateur* down and removed the gloves. When I took off the black broad-brimmed hat and went to hand it to Monsieur Ladoux he said, *"Ça c'est pour vous maintenant."* He smiled at me. I felt as though I had just earned a badge of some sort. I limped home and took a hot bath. While I was soaking in the tub, Tabitha walked in. She curled up on my soiled clothing and went to sleep.

The next day our doorbell sounded and I walked down to find Monsieur Ladoux there with two cases of wine. *"C'est pour vous. Merci de votre assistance."*

I thanked him profusely and said it wasn't necessary, but he said it was and he insisted on showing his appreciation.

After he left, I opened one of the cases and lifted out a bottle. The red wine was ten years old and ready to drink. I carried the cases into the wine cellar. Then, taking one bottle upstairs I called, "Marie-Hélène, come and look at this."

We had already planned a leg of lamb roasted in rosemary for dinner that night. I opened the bottle early to let it breathe, and then just before we sat down at the table I poured two glasses. We stood in the kitchen tasting the wine. The tannins had faded, leaving firm structure and a velvet texture for the abundance of fruit. This was far better than a *vin de pays*. The *terroir* of the southern Rhône pervaded the wine.

"Monsieur Ladoux knows his wines," Marie-Hélène said, looking into her glass. "This will be a perfect match for the lamb. After all, both come from the hills of Provence."

• • •

My calls to the electrician seemed futile and we began to consider hiring someone else to finish the work. For unknown reasons we stayed the course and continued trying to reach Monsieur Faret. He seemed to have fallen off the planet. Earlier this spring he had roughed in the wiring for the guest suite. The other trades had done their part by laying the floor tiles, putting up the plasterboard on the walls and ceiling, and plumbing the new bathroom. I had painted the walls. The bathroom shower was tiled. The furniture was in place. However, there was no electricity.

"We received an e-mail from Beth this morning. It seems Paris was good for them and they've reconciled," Marie-Hélène said over coffee.

"Oh," I said, lifting my eyes from the *Herald Tribune*.

"In fact, they are planning a second honeymoon in Hawaii."

"That's good news."

"Yes," Marie-Hélène said, pouring more coffee.

"Well, you know, I sent an e-mail to the office yesterday."

Marie-Hélène looked over at me, waiting for the rest of the information.

"I said that I wanted to retire soon and the firm should start thinking about the changes that need to be made."

Marie-Hélène stared at me. "I thought you were wedded to that law firm."

"So did I. But I guess some things have changed."

"Are you ready for this?"

"Yes, my partners and I just have to work out the steps and set the date."

Marie-Hélène leaned over and kissed me on the cheek.

Chapter 16
Christening a folly

"CONNIE CALLED. They have a group at their cooking school this week and want to take them to Villeperdrix for some country food. She wants to know if we would like to join them."

"Where is that?" I asked.

"It's a village in the hills somewhere. She says we could all go in their van. Tom knows the way. Apparently the place has genuine country charm. It's great for their visitors as they can see a real *provençal* country restaurant. It sounds like fun."

We drove over to the Williams' home. Tom opened the massive wooden gates and we parked in their enclosed garden. We were ready to go, so after a round of introductions everyone but me climbed into the van and Tom drove out. I closed the gates behind us.

Tom and Connie were natural tourist guides, telling us all about the plan for the evening.

"The restaurant is in a remote village called Villeperdrix,"

Tom explained. "It sounds like it comes from *perdre*, meaning 'lost,' which seems so appropriate considering the place is in the middle of nowhere. But in fact *'perdrix'* is a partridge. Many of the places around here have descriptive names. 'Vinsobres' means sober wines; 'Dieulefit' means made by God; 'Rochebrune' is a brown rock outcropping; 'Mont Ventoux' is the windy mountain."

Connie continued. "The restaurant is in an old olive *moulin*. The huge stone grinding wheel still sits in the middle of the room. Madame only opens for business if it suits her and there are sufficient people coming to make it worth her while to cook. She won't say in advance what she will be serving. There's no menu. The food simply arrives at the table. She says most of it comes from her own farm. I think she just looks around to see what she has that day. She wants the reservation made a day ahead. The first time we came she served fresh lamb."

After a half-hour drive, Tom turned off onto a steep narrow road leading up a rocky hill. Apart from the road, there was no evidence of human activity to be seen in the area. Another fifteen minutes of driving brought us to a tiny village on a hilltop. I looked around and could see only hills to the horizon in all directions. A small grove of walnut trees stood next to the church.

Tom pulled up beside another vehicle and we all climbed out. There was no evidence of a restaurant anywhere.

"It's right there," Tom said, pointing at a stone building.

I still couldn't see a sign. We walked over and Tom opened the door. We all filed into a dimly lit room with a low, vaulted stone ceiling. The stone wheel occupied the centre of the room. Two large wood-plank tables ran down the sides of the room and a few smaller tables occupied the corners.

A stout woman with meaty peasant hands, wearing a patterned frock and an apron, approached us.

Tom immediately turned and walked over to her. "Madame!" he exclaimed, opening his arms in pleasure. She responded to his show of warmth and welcomed him. He then introduced all of us to her. She smiled with delight. As we seated ourselves at one of the large tables, she went off to the kitchen. Moments later she returned with two large jugs of wine.

"Tonight I have a warm chicken-liver salad and rabbit ragout," she announced. Then she turned and walked away to the kitchen again.

This time she returned with two bowls of salad. We were to serve ourselves.

Tom waited for her to go back to the kitchen before saying in a lowered voice, "Make sure you only take what you can eat. If you don't finish what's on your plate she will wait for you to do so, or even ask why you didn't like it."

When she saw that we all had finished our plates she came back and looked in the salad bowls. "You need to finish *la salade*," she said. We all looked a bit sheepish and took more. Meanwhile she was refilling the jugs on the table with wine.

The rabbit ragout arrived in a large iron pot brimful of steaming dark brown sauce and rabbit. The aroma had us waiting to be served. She ladled it onto the plates and set them one by one in front of us. Before returning to the kitchen she looked to see if more wine was needed.

She must have had the ragout braising for hours, as the meat was so tender it fell away from the bones.

Every now and then a high-pitched voice yelled out stridently in the kitchen, above the conversation in the restaurant.

Finally, curious, I asked Marie-Hélène, "What is she saying?"

"I can't understand her. She's speaking an unusual patois."

We finished all the rabbit, to the pleasure of Madame, who was smiling. We had also consumed copious quantities of wine.

Dessert simply arrived without anyone asking. It was a bread pudding with ground walnuts sprinkled on top.

Without clearing the dessert dishes from the table, Madame came back with eight small glasses and a bottle containing a murky green liquid. She poured the glasses, handed one to each of us and waited for us to taste it. The flavour was rosemary. It was obvious that we had to tell her what we thought. It was in fact very good.

Tom picked up on what she was waiting for and said, *"Madame, c'est une boisson extraordinaire!"* He raised his hands in the air and turned to look at her.

She broke into another smile and poured more.

We were all relaxed and carrying on an animated conversation when I heard the same loud voice from the kitchen again. Just then a very elderly lady, cane in hand, emerged, walked the length of the restaurant and headed out the front door. She crossed the street, and through the windows we watched her enter the building on the other side. She must have been the *maman,* departing when her work was done for the evening.

As we prepared to leave, we settled the bill. It was fifteen euros each, and cash only.

Tom and Connie were thanking Madame effusively at the door when she walked over to the table we had sat at and picked up the half-full bottle of her liqueur. She came back and put the bottle in the crook of Tom's arm.

"C'est pour vous, Monsieur."

"Non, non. Ce n'est pas possible, Madame!" Tom protested.

"Voui, pour vous."

. . .

Marie-Hélène and I decided it was time to solve the problem of the missing electrician. I was having no luck with my calls to Monsieur Faret.

"Okay," Marie-Hélène said, "he is probably too busy with other, bigger jobs. Furthermore, he doesn't want to return our calls because he will be embarrassed. We've already learned that French artisans avoid saying no to a request. Leave it to me."

At one o'clock the next day, just when everyone would be at lunch, I overheard Marie-Hélène talking on the telephone. She walked onto the balcony.

"I just spoke to Monsieur Faret."

"How did you manage that?" I asked with amazement.

"Well, I knew he would be home for lunch, so I called him there. When he answered, I told him that we would be leaving for Canada next week, and that the suite was finished except for the wiring. We would really like to pay him for all the work he has done so far, but as the wiring isn't complete we will pay him next year when we return."

"And . . . ?"

"He says he'll be here *tomorrow morning*."

We were up early the next day and waiting. Monsieur Faret's van came up the road and turned into our driveway. The greetings were as warm as for long-lost friends. Then he and his assistant got to work.

A new breaker box was fitted next to the existing one and more wiring was run in place. Electrical boxes and outlets went in and were tested. Switches were installed, as were recessed ceiling lights. The breakers were connected and the system checked. Cover plates were screwed in place and sconces mounted on the walls. By eleven-thirty that morning, the wiring was complete.

Monsieur Faret took time to show off the new lighting system and to have a social chat. Then he made a quick trot out to his van for the bill that was already prepared. We wrote a cheque, and after all the proper thanks and handshakes, he looked at his watch and said it was time for lunch. He and his assistant loaded their tools in the van and were off. The timing had been impeccable.

We stood in our new guest suite marvelling at the finished product.

I turned to Marie-Hélène. "You work miracles."

"I know. So do you think we deserve a nice lunch in Vaison today?"

"I'm in."

"Okay, *allons-y.*"

Vaison is just twenty minutes away, so we got there in time to get an outdoor table under the awning and a towering plane tree. Chez Pascal is a gem of a *bistrot.*

"I'll have a *salade de chèvre chaude,*" Marie-Hélène said without looking at the menu.

I scanned the posted *menu du jour.* "The *poulet en jus avec gratin* looks good."

When the wine arrived Marie-Hélène raised her glass. "I think we need a toast to this morning. . . . Here's to another project finished!"

We did more than that, for we took the rest of the afternoon to enjoy lunch, and then we returned home to carry the furniture into the guest suite.

•   •   •

At the Thursday market a few weeks later we met Madame Joule on the street.

"Pierre Luc's sale has fallen through. The Belgians changed their minds and walked away from their deposit. He lost the sale but has got something out of it."

"Do you mean to say that he made money by not selling?"

"Yes. After my commission, he will get the rest of the deposit. He has been very, very lucky." I thought about Fanny and Violette and agreed.

We continued walking about the market, buying food at the stalls we preferred, when I noticed a computer store that had just opened. We stopped and looked in the window at all the latest technology, then went inside.

The young man behind the counter smiled. *"Bonjour, Monsieur, Dame Bitney."*

I was taken aback because I had never seen this person before. He picked up on my surprise and laughed.

"Pardonnez-moi." And then in perfect English he went on, "I'm Marius Buisson, your neighbour. You haven't seen me before without my helmet on."

Standing nearby was an attractive young woman in black leathers. "This is my *petite amie,* Angèle. What is the expression in English?"

"Beautiful companion or girlfriend," I replied, smiling.

We congratulated them on the new store and talked for a while, then left to finish our shopping.

Marie-Hélène said, "This is a *very* prolific country."

I didn't grasp her statement. "What?" I asked.

"Well, did you see her?" Marie-Hélène inquired,

"Yes, of course, we just met her. It was hard not to do so. She's very pretty."

"That's not what I meant. Her leather jacket doesn't fit around the chest."

I hesitated now, trying to grasp the fashion comment.

"She's pregnant. They've come into a home just in time."

* * *

Some say the mistral wind starts in Russia and sweeps down the Rhône Valley gathering force until it blows itself out in the Mediterranean. The force of the wind ravages everything in its path, leaving trees permanently bent toward the south, tiles torn off rooftops and hurled like projectiles, and a population in a state of unrest. The *vent du sud* is a different wind. It comes from the south off the Mediterranean and hits like a mariner's gale, bringing storms with it. Both winds arrive with bitter violence. As the mistral is considered the worse of the two, most houses are built on the south slope of the hills to gain protection. This in turn leaves them exposed to the *vent du sud*.

I had wondered why the houses all had shutters, which seemed rather quaint and old-fashioned. Then Jean telephoned one afternoon and said a mistral was forecast overnight and we should close all the windows and shutters. By the time we went to bed, the wind was picking up force. We thought little of it until every gust of wind brought shrill whistling through the gaps around the doors and windows. The tightly fastened shutters set up a discordant clattering din. I got up to check if they were properly fastened and when I opened the window I was hit with a gale. Even with the shutters closed the wind blew in. Yes, the shutters were fastened, but I had an image of one being torn from its hinges and sent flying in the wind. Sleep that night was impossible. The house almost shook with the gusts, and we heard the iron patio furniture clattering and then colliding with something in the yard.

By daybreak the wind had blown itself out and we had finally fallen asleep. We slept on into the morning until the telephone rang.

"Hello?" Marie-Hélène said sleepily.

"C'est Suzette. Is everything alright?"

"Yes," Marie-Hélène said, "we just didn't get much sleep last night. Why do you ask?"

"Well we saw that your shutters are still closed, so we thought we should call."

We opened the shutters to bright sunlight. The mistral had swept away all the clouds and only blue sky remained.

Jean later told us about the time he was closing his garage door in the wind when a gust swung it out of his grasp and it hit him, breaking his shoulder. "That was a very small wind last night," he said. "The record mistral lasted over a hundred days." We had a better appreciation for the rocks that we had seen on the tiled rooftops and the heavy wood shutters that fit tightly in place.

One morning nearly two weeks after François had delivered the stones, I looked out the bedroom window at the ragged wall and the pile of stones. My body had healed from the earlier work, and I put on a pair of shorts, T-shirt and a pair of old boots, found my work gloves and walked out into the garden with a cup of coffee. When the cup was empty, I had already mentally fitted a half-dozen stones into place. By noon several new courses of stones had raised the height of the wall by another two feet. By dinnertime it was half-built, and Marie-Hélène came out with two glasses of wine. That was my signal to stop working. I took off my gloves and accepted the glass she offered me. We stood looking at the wall. It was suddenly taking shape.

Over the next days the wall rose to the height of the patio, and then the flat stones capped it off six inches higher.

"All I need is a load of earth to fill in behind the wall, and gravel on top of that to extend the existing patio over to the wall."

Marie-Hélène looked at it. "Let's plant a boxwood hedge along the top of the wall. It will offer more privacy from the road and nicely edge the patio."

A call was made to François. He arrived the next Friday with a load of earth, gravel and even the boxwood shrubs. Between the two of us, we moved the earth, spread gravel and planted the boxwood. Then we carried the wrought-iron table and chairs over and set them in the middle of the new patio.

Marie-Hélène appeared with a bottle of sparkling *rosé* and three flutes. I popped the cork and poured the wine. We sat and drank a toast to my once-absurd folly, now finally completed.

Departure
One last dinner

BUSY WORKING under the shade of an oak tree in the garden in late September, I hadn't seen Pierre Luc coming down the road.

"*Salut,*" he called out. I turned to see him and his dog standing next to our fence.

"*Bonjour,*" I replied as we shook hands. "*Comment ça va?*"

"I'm well. Isn't it a nice day?"

This was unusual for Pierre Luc, so I took a closer look. He was clean-shaven and he wasn't wearing his normal bar clothes. Then I saw the dog. It had been washed and brushed recently. I was now curious. "So where are you off to? Isn't it a bit early for your friends at Bar des Amis?"

"*Beh, oui.* But I won't have time to see them today. I'm going to Nyons Nature to order some fertilizer for the orchard. It will give the trees a start for next year. There's no money in apricots, but it's still worth doing."

His manner had changed. I listened, looking at him. He

must have felt my eyes on him because he hesitated and then continued.

"My father and his friend up the hill tried growing an obscure variety of grape years ago. It failed miserably, and they both nearly went broke. They just scraped by. Nobody wanted the grapes. There was no money to replant, so the vines just stayed there and the grapes were sold off for blending." He stopped to light a cigarette before continuing.

"Last month the owner of a famous château up north wanted to buy his vineyard but the man's haughty manner put him off. My father's friend says that this variety—Viognier—has become popular and is selling well. Between us we have over two hectares of mature old vines. He's too old, but he'll let me be the tenant farmer of his vines for a share of the profit."

This did not sound like the Pierre Luc that I knew, so I asked, "Do you really want to do this? It sounds like a lot of work."

"Well, Fanny is back with Violette and I've got to make a go of it. I don't want to disappoint her again. She wants to see something succeed for a change."

"So you're going to start a boutique winery on your own without AOC status."

He already had the answer to this. "AOC is old stuff and stifles new ideas in winemaking. The local guys are finding it hard to sell their grapes these days as the market is flooded with the AOC wines from around here." He punctuated his sentence with a deep draw on his cigarette. "But the boutique wineries have people lined up at their doors waiting to buy. The money is in unique, small-volume, well-made varietals these days. Fanny's brother in Rochebrune has a press, vats, bottling equipment, everything. All I have to do is buy my own vats and barrels."

"Sounds pretty adventurous," I threw in.

"What have I got to lose?"

"Your farm."

"*Bof*—I almost lost it anyway. I've got a little money now, and Crédit Agricole will lend me enough to drill a well to irrigate the vineyards. The government subsidy will cover the interest cost on the money. Besides, Fanny has enrolled at l'Université du Vin de Suze-la-Rousse this fall, and I grew up tending vines."

I walked back indoors looking for Marie-Hélène. "Pierre Luc is a new man. It's as if a spark has ignited in him."

After the harvesting of the grapes in the vineyards the weather turned cooler and mushrooms started to appear in the forests. Mushrooms of all sizes and colours, still fresh and muddy, turned up on stall tables in the Thursday market. *Champignons* are taken seriously in France. Of the more than 3,000 varieties found in France, only a few are safe to eat. Some thirty people die each year from mushroom poisoning. Needless to say, there is an emergency services number—*urgences!*—available to call.

The *librairie* had changed its window display to books on mushrooms, and the pharmacy put out a sign stating that they would look at any mushrooms brought in to them to confirm whether they were poisonous or nonpoisonous.

There are rules on how to pick. For instance, the mushrooms must be of a certain size to be sure they have released their spores for propagation. The only tool to be used is a knife to cleanly cut off the cap without damaging the base. Furthermore, the mushrooms must be carried in a wicker basket so that the spores can fall through to the ground, encouraging propagation.

Late one afternoon we drove up Garde Grosse, the mountain across the valley from our house that we looked out on each day.

Hikers were coming out of the trails onto the road with sacks filled with the mushrooms they had gathered in the forest.

In our garden, small grey growths began to spring up at the base of a few trees and elsewhere. They appeared almost overnight and—if not picked—within a day or two began to shrivel away. I asked Jean if they were edible.

"Not the small ones there, but these grey ones at the base of this tree are. They are called *la mat.*"

"How should we prepare them?" I asked.

"Pick them and leave them on the fence between our yards. I'll ask Suzette to do it."

The fence between our properties had become a clearing house for exchanging things.

The next day I left a bag hanging on the fence and we went out for the afternoon. When we returned, the bag had changed. It now contained a pot of beautifully prepared mushrooms. At dinner that evening, we revelled in the mushrooms from our garden.

I placed the bag with the empty pot on the fence and it was gone the following day.

Jean had telephoned that day and suggested another hike before we left for the fall. This time we would drive up the Montagne des Vaux to the north of Nyons and hike into the Forêt Domaniale de Vaux.

The three of us climbed into Jean's tiny Peugeot and drove off in the cool morning air. The mountain rises 600 metres over the valley floor and is the first real evidence of the Pre-Alps. The road took us partway up the mountain and came to an end. We parked and got out, put on our warmer clothing and shouldered our knapsacks. From here the trail was uphill for a considerable distance into the trees before it levelled along the crest. The trees were relatively young, and stumps protruded from the rocky soil. Along the trail we passed the ruins of small stone structures.

Jean pointed at the ruins. "When the forest was logged, the workers built kilns to make charcoal. Mules would carry the charcoal down to the nearby villages, where it would be sold to those who could afford it. Everyone else burned whatever they could cut on their own land or buy from the wood merchants. The cutting devastated the slopes and over the years since then, reforestation programs have been carried out."

Fortunately almost a hundred years had passed, so the new-growth forests were well established.

As we reached the mountain ridge the next valley came into view. It was a remote area, sparsely populated with only a few farmhouses and outbuildings. A troupe of sheep was foraging on a hillside across the valley, their white coats standing out from the pale greenery, their movements hardly detectable in the distance. All the same, we could hear their bells in the calm air.

We built up body heat on the upward hike and had to take off a layer of clothing. By noon the air was warm and the knapsacks felt heavier. When we arrived at a rock promontory, Jean said we should stop for lunch. Our feet dangled out in space while we took in the panoramic view. To the east were the wild Pre-Alps with the snow-capped Alps in the distance, and to the west lay the broad plain of the Rhône Valley. While Jean and Marie-Hélène chatted in French, I took in the warmth of the fall sun and faced the fact that we would be returning to Canada in a few weeks.

We started back along a different forest trail, heavily treed with dense vegetation. Each step required our concentration so that we wouldn't trip over the exposed roots or loose rocks. We were walking in silence, watching our feet so intently that we hadn't paid attention to the trail ahead. Jean was in the lead when he froze and motioned with his hand for us to stop. We stood still without saying a word. Fifty metres ahead a mature wild boar trotted toward us on the trail. Behind was a string of piglets, all pale beige and striped like chipmunks, and then at the rear the mother. The male—with a massive head and shoulders tapering toward the hindquarters—must have sensed us, for he stopped and raised his huge head in the air. His tusks and hair protruded on either side like a handlebar moustache. He seemed to be assessing what to do. The bristles down his back stood up like a mane. The group had taken his lead and all remained motionless. Then suddenly he stepped from the path and they disappeared into the underbrush.

Jean waited and said nothing for at least a minute. Then he turned and smiled. "They've gone. . . . That was unusual. Wild boars are very prolific in these forests, but they are generally nocturnal."

He sat down on a rock before continuing. "A group of wild boar is called a 'sounder.' Those piglets were small for this time of year. That must be a late litter. The male doesn't normally stay with the litter and moves on. This one hasn't, for some reason. He was a big one, close to 200 kilos."

Jean's eyes lit up. "Did you see the tusks? They grow from both the upper and lower canines and curve upward. The upper tusks act as sharpening tools for the lower tusks—they become almost razor sharp."

I interrupted to ask, "Why did the male hesitate so long before leaving the trail?"

"He probably heard or smelled us first. But boar have poor eyesight—so he stood there trying to assess the situation, deciding what to do. Generally they are wary of people and are not aggressive unless attacked or cornered. The mother will be more so to protect her young."

"Are they dangerous?" I asked in a low voice.

Jean made a slicing motion across his leg indicating what the tusks could do. "They can move at speeds over forty kilometres per hour. That male could inflict a ten-centimetre gash over five centimetres deep."

We walked toward the spot on the trail, watching to see if the boars were visible in the undergrowth, but they had gone. As we continued along the path I couldn't help looking over my shoulder from time to time.

After a few minutes, we felt more relieved and the conversation picked up again.

"Jean says that these trails lead to other villages many kilometres away," Marie-Hélène translated for me. Jean spoke faster the more he talked.

"Apparently during the French Revolution some of the nobility moved to Nyons as it is remote and on the foothills of the Alps. They feared being arrested and guillotined."

Ever physically expressive, Jean made another slicing motion with his hand, this time at his neck.

"If the Revolutionary Guard came looking for them, in a matter of minutes they could hike into the forests on these mountains, coming out in a distant village."

Marie-Hélène said, "Oh, Gordon, do you recall the first house we looked at in the old section of Nyons? The iron railing on the staircase had a family crest and initials. The date of construction carved in the stonework was 1794—just five years after the revolution began."

It took over an hour to emerge onto the roadway. The red roofs of Nyons lay below us, looking peaceful in the sheltered valley.

To the south, Montagne Garde Grosse rose 944 metres. The Eygues River cut a meandering path through the village and on toward the Rhône Valley. We could see the hillside where our house sat amid the scattered patches of vineyards and orchards. Beyond, to the west, lay the vast plain of the valley and the silver streak of the Rhône River flowing south to the Mediterranean. The sun beat on our faces as we stood there pointing out familiar landmarks to each other. The drive home took minutes, and after showering we walked next door for one of Suzette's extraordinary multi-course dinners.

The meal began with asparagus served on a poached egg, followed by ratatouille. The main course, *faisan rotis*, was served with two pheasant feathers protruding upward from the wings and accompanied by *pommes dauphine* enriched with Bayonne ham. Jean showed off his wine cellar by bringing up a bottle so old the label was illegible. The printing on the cork gave away the contents as Gigondas. The wine was so smooth and softened by age it could have come from anywhere. For dessert Suzette presented a *tarte aux figues*. To conclude the dinner, Jean brought out a highly alcoholic home-made *digestif* infused with a bitter mountain herb called *génépi*.

· · ·

We had begun to accept that our summer in Provence was again coming to an end. Winter was fast approaching, and our obligations in Vancouver were waiting for us. It was time to bring out suitcases and Tabitha's travelling case. We put Myrtille and the kittens in their wicker basket and Marie-Hélène held it while I drove down the hill to Yvette and Gilles' home. Yvette was there, so she took the basket and its meowing contents indoors and then came back out. She smiled.

"Les vacances d'été de Myrtille sont terminés."

We laughed and exchanged hugs.

"Bon retour au Canada. Au printemps!" she said, and we laughed again.

Closing up the house for the winter diverted our attention from the reality that we were leaving. At last the water was drained from the plumbing system, the fridge emptied and the door propped open, the garden furniture brought into the garage and then the personal packing done. The next morning we closed all the shutters and locked the door. We drove out of the driveway and then stopped to lock the gate behind us as the final task of autumn. We promised ourselves that next spring we would be back to stay even longer.

Afterword

Tabitha (a.k.a. Minou) now resides with us in Vancouver and no longer travels to France. Myrtille still lives in Nyons with her family and roams the same hillside. She visits the villa *Les Oliviers* from time to time. Nyons continues to prosper, and the orchards bear their fruit and olives each year.

The factory in the village sends out its scented clouds of smoke each summer as it distils the lavender to make concentrated essences. It is fed by the fields that carpet the countryside like broad swathes of blue corduroy.

A communist was elected to the village council, but nothing seemed to come of that. Jacques Chirac is no longer the President of France. Nicolas Sarkozy is now in the Élysée Palace, with plans for shaking up the system.

Lydie Marshall continues to write cookbooks on regional French cuisine from her château in Nyons.

The *atelier* on our hillside still creates fine mohair products from just one silky-blond mohair goat.

Pierre Luc Paysan has become a successful *vigneron*, making a unique boutique wine from his Viognier grapes, and his wife tends their apricot orchard. Their green Citröen 2CV is gone, replaced by a more practical farm truck.

Marius Buisson and his *belle amie* are raising a son. His computer store is thriving. The villagers of Nyons have moved online and have better access to the outside world than René Barjavel enjoyed with the train service.

The second honeymoon of Beth and her husband was a success, and they have now started a family in Vancouver. Doug and Dot Mallard and their children made it safely home, and Doug continues to use the services of my former law firm.

For most of the people of Nyons life goes on as ever, some things changing, some staying the same.

As for me, I retired from law and am now reading the great French literature of Victor Hugo, Alexandre Dumas and Colette, and of course the superb mysteries of the extraordinarily prolific Georges Simenon. My taste for cheeses and sausages continues to broaden. I have not worked in a vineyard since helping M. Ladoux, and I have not built another dry stone wall.

—Gordon Bitney

Outdoor Markets *(Les Marchés)* in and around Nyons

Monday *(Lundi)*
  Bédoin
  Bollène
  Tulette

Tuesday *(Mardi)*
  Mondragon
  Avignon
  Caromb
  Grignan
  Aix-en-Provence
  Vaison-la-Romaine

Wednesday *(Mercredi)*
  Avignon
  Arles
  Malaucène
  Valréas
  Buis les Baronnies
  Montélimar

Thursday *(Jeudi)*
  Nyons
  Cairanne
  Aubignan
  Orange
  Avignon
  Aix-en-Provence
  Rochegude

Friday *(Vendredi)*
  Carpentras
  Avignon
  Taulignan
  Suze-la-Rousse
  Châteauneuf-du-Pape
  Dieulefit

Saturday *(Samedi)*
  Bollène
  Avignon
  Arles
  Grillon
  Montèlimar
  Richerenches
  Valrèas
  Aix-en-Provence

Sunday *(Dimanche)*
  Avignon
  Isle-sur-la-Sorgue
  Mirabeau
  Jonquières

Colombet
53 Place de la Libération, Nyons.
A traditional hotel

Le Petit Caveau
9 rue Victor Hugo, Nyons
Cuisine of the area

La Belle Epoque
25 Place de la Libération, Nyons.
Brasserie

La charrette bleue
Exit Les Pilles, route to Gap D94
Traditional cuisine

L'Oliveraie
on the route from Nyons to Orange
Pizzas, salads at poolside

Auberge du Petit Bistrot
Place de l'Eglise, Vinsobres
French bistrot cuisine

Ayme Truffes
Domain de Bramarel, 26230, Grignan
Truffles

Ferme-Auberge Le Moulin du Château
Villeperdrix, 20 km north-east of Nyons
Farm fare

Mohair du Moulin
Le Moulin, 26110 Saint-Sauveur-Gouvernet.
Mohair artisan

Coopérative de Nyonsais
Place Olivier de Serres, Nyons
Olives, olive oil, tapenade, wines

Moulin Ramade
7 impasse du Moulin, avenue Paul Laurens, Nyons
Olives, olive oil, tapenade

Les Deux Garçons
Cours Mirabeau, Aix-en-Provence
Traditional French cuisine

Café Verdun
Place de Verdun, Aix-en-Provence.
Café

La Beaugravière
RN7 Mondragon
Haute cuisine, truffle menu, extraordinary wine cellar

Chez Nane
7 avenue des 4-Otageson, beside the canal at the back of an antique warehouse, Isle-sur-la-Sorgue
Café

Chez Pascal
12 Place Montfort, Vaison-la-Romaine
Bistrot

BONNES ADRESSES

La Mirande
4 Place de La Mirande, Avignon
Haute cuisine, hotel

Le Bercail
Ile de la Barthelasse, Avignon
Café

La Cour du Louvre
23 rue Saint Agricol, Avignon
Restaurant

L'oustalet
Gigondas
Traditional French cuisine

Le Brin d'Olivier
4 rue du Ventoux, Vaison-la-Romaine
Excellent cuisine

La Fontaine
in Le Beffroi Hostellerie, rue de l'Évêché, Cité Médiévale, Vaison-la-Romaine
Restaurant

Chez Gilbert
the Port, Cassis
Bouillabaisse

Gordon Bitney spent thirty years practising law in Vancouver until he retired. He and his wife bought a villa in Provence and lived between there and Vancouver with their cats. The way of life in the village of Nyons inspired this book.